The Best Nutrition Plan Of 2022

Hannah W. Dotson

Contents

Chapter One

INTRODUCTION

The focus of this concise book is on working smart to get the outcomes you actually want out of your life. A lot of time and effort might be saved if individuals learned more about their bodies and how they operate in the direction of their goals. Those who have the desire to work hard to achieve their ideal physique and are seeking for the most efficient approach to do it may benefit from these ideas and guidance. Those who don't want to "beat about the bush," are looking for the greatest quality, or have tried to accomplish their fitness objective several times but haven't seen substantial gains may find this book incredibly valuable.. There are no more excuses for these readers, and this guide will help them take charge of their fitness.

In this book, you'll learn all you need to know about how to burn fat and develop muscle while maintaining a healthy lifestyle. This book is mostly focused on nutrition since working out without paying attention to what you eat can lead to disappointing outcomes. My job is to teach individuals that they don't have to restrict themselves to a specific diet in order to achieve their goals. To have the body you want, you need to know how to get rid of the behaviours that aren't required and focus on the ones that are. Beginners, as well as those with some training experience who want to learn more about nutrition and training, will benefit greatly from this information because it will cut down on the time it takes to accomplish any fitness objective. There are clear headings for each part, and the information is presented in a style that is easy to follow. Think of this book as a road map and essential tool for achieving your ideal physical appearance. The only thing left to do after reading this book is to put in the effort to achieve your objective.

Believing you can is half the battle won. According to Theodore Roosevelt

In this context, "optimal" means "best," "most favourable," or "preferred."

There is always a better or more efficient approach to accomplish your aim. In order to get the best possible outcomes in terms of diet and exercise, this guide is here to help. For those who aren't familiar with fitness terminology, this material will assist them comprehend the fundamentals of fat burning and muscle building. You may achieve your fitness goals in the quickest and most effective manner by following this easy instructions. With the information you've just learned, you may attack your objective with complete self-awareness and self-assurance.

FOOD INTIMACY

"A thousand-mile voyage, "

"it all starts with one small step" the great lama

Chapter Two

TIPS

In the battle between eating healthily and reaching your fitness goals, which do you choose?

People immediately think of healthy food when they think about getting a terrific body. Although eating healthily does not guarantee that you'll achieve your ideal body, it can help you get there. Achieving the body of your dreams does not necessarily indicate that you are eating a healthy diet. When you eat healthfully, you're giving your body the nourishment it needs to perform at its best. For optimal health, your body requires a certain balance of micro-nutrients and macro-nutrients (fat, protein and carbohydrate) in your diet. Maintaining good health is your your duty, not someone else's. In order to have a well-defined physique, one must either reduce body fat or increase muscular mass. When you're trying to lose weight, your body has to be in a calorie deficit, which means burning more calories than you consume each day. To gain weight, you must consume more calories than you expend, which is called a calorie surplus.

Eating healthily has several advantages, but it is as crucial to meet your fitness objective. Consuming 10,000 calories of veggies a day is a healthy diet, but it isn't enough to help you lose weight if your objective is to burn fat. This means that a healthy diet and exercise plan can help you achieve your desired weight and maintain a healthy lifestyle. Both of these goals may be achieved by eating enough calories to meet your fitness goals while also ensuring that you get enough micronutrients and macronutrients to keep your body healthy and functioning properly.

A CALORIE IS AN INDIVIDUAL CALORIE.

Calories are a term you hear a lot, but what exactly do they mean? A calorie is a unit of measurement for the amount of energy in a substance. When you consume, the amount of energy it contains, not its mass, is what matters most. How much energy your body can acquire from eating or drinking anything that has 100 calories is referred to as the calorie count. If you think about how much gas is poured into a car, you'll realise that the quantity of calories you consume is counted in grammes. Calories are a measure of how much energy your body will receive from the food or drink you consume since each meal or drink you consume is broken down differently by your body. The term "calorie" simply refers to "energy."

Calories: Good or Bad for You?

Since your body need calories for energy, they are not harmful to your diet. Eating too many calories and not doing enough physical exercise might contribute to weight gain in the long run. Consuming too little calories over a long period of time might have a severe impact on your health. Lettuce, on the other hand, contains just 10 calories per cup, whereas peanuts have 427 calories per half cup. You can make better dietary choices if you know how many calories you require each day.

Your body uses calories in a variety of ways.

Calories are required by your body only to keep you alive and keep you functioning normally. For example, it's utilised to maintain your heart pumping and lungs breathing. Every cell in your body relies on calories to perform its fundamental and complicated activities, including the control of your body temperature. The more calories you burn by being active, the better. A calorie-rich diet is necessary for your body's continual growth and development. When you eat, when you rest, and even when you sleep, your body burns calories without you even noticing.

HOW MANY CALORIES ARE YOU USING NOW?

The quantity of calories a person needs to consume depends on a variety of factors, including their weight and metabolism. Among these indicators include a person's height and weight as well as their age and degree of daily physical activity. The larger a person is, the more calories they may require, and the opposite is also true. It's possible for two persons with the same body proportions to have vastly differing calorie needs because of the way their bodies process food. The number of calories your body requires may be calculated using calorie calculators that can be found online. Extra calories are stored as fat if consumed in excess of what your body requires. A person's body will turn to fat reserves for energy if they consume less calories than they require. You can better regulate your weight if you know how many calories you require.

BASICS AT THE GLOBAL LEVEL

Carbohydrates, lipids, and protein are macronutrients or macros. The term "macro" refers to a nutrient that is substantial enough to produce calories (the only other substance that provides calories is alcohol but is not a macronutrient since we do not need it for survival). These three macronutrients are the building blocks of all food. The food you eat is not recognised as "chicken, rice, salad, etc." by your body. Your body, on the other hand, interprets everything you eat as either a carbohydrate, fat, or protein. These macronutrients are listed in bold on the nutrition label of any food or beverage product because of this.

A CARB IS WHAT?

When it comes to fuel, carbohydrates are the most important. Carbohydrates can be divided into simple and complicated varieties. The energy you get from a simple carbohydrate is short-lived. Because it takes your body longer to digest a complex carb, it provides you with more energy for longer periods of time. It doesn't matter if you eat basic or complex carbs. Both of these strategies may be put to good use at any time of the day. When you get up in the morning, it's likely that you haven't eaten in the past few hours. As a result, consuming simple carbohydrates for quick energy may be a wise decision. Carbohydrates, especially complex carbohydrates, are an excellent choice for those who will be out of the house for an extended period of time. As a result, by including both complex and simple carbohydrates in your diet, you may better regulate your energy levels throughout the day.

Some examples of complex carbohydrates include meals like whole grains like whole wheat bread and brown rice, along with sweet potatoes and legumes. Fruits, white bread, white rice, white potatoes, veggies, juice, pop tarts, etc. are all examples of simple carbohydrates. Glucose, fructose, lactose, sucrose, and other types of sugar are all examples of a simple carbohydrate. Both simple and complex carbohydrates are eventually converted to sugar in the body, but digestion and absorption are the primary distinctions between the two.

Protein is a type of macromolecule that consists of chains of amino acids linked together into

Protein aids in tissue growth and repair, as well as a variety of cellular processes. It is essential for the growth of hair, nails, muscle, and other body components. Proteins are constructed from amino acids. A protein is deemed incomplete if it lacks one or more of its 20 amino acids; a complete protein has all of these amino acids. Meats such as chicken, cattle, steak, and fish, as well as eggs, milk, and whey protein, are the primary sources of complete proteins. Grain, nut and seed-based foods, as well as legumes and nuts, are considered inadequate proteins. 0.8 to 1.2 grammes of protein per pound of body weight is suggested for maximum muscular building. Muscle development and repair can be aided by any complete protein, regardless of the kind, source, absorption rate, or filtering technique. However, the benefits of a complete protein can't be overestimated when it comes to muscle development or repair. The most important thing is to obtain enough protein to meet your body's needs for growth.

WHAT IS FAT ABOUT?

When fat is present in the body, hormones are controlled, cells are transported, and other nutrients are able to carry out their functions in the body. When it comes to energy, fat is your body's second-biggest source. In the absence of carbohydrates, your body will turn to fat as a source of energy. Because of this, fat loss is based on cutting back on primary energy sources (carbs) so that the body can utilise its secondary energy source (fat) (body fat). Saturated, polyunsaturated, monounsaturated, and trans-fats are all kinds of fats that may be found in food. You should avoid trans-fat because of its detrimental effects on your health. While there are advantages and disadvantages to each kind of fat, the total amount of fat in a food is an important consideration. Foods with a lot of fat in them include butter, peanut butter, oils, avocado, and other nuts and seeds. Even if you're attempting to lose weight, it's crucial to obtain enough fat in your diet to keep your hormones in balance. Depending on the person and their fitness goals, the daily fat requirement might range from 15% to over 40% of total calories.

What's the use of keeping track of macros?

THE QUALITY OF YOUR WEIGHT LOSS OR WEIGHT GAIN

You will lose weight if you are in a calorie deficit, which means you are burning more calories than you are taking in. This does not guarantee that you will lose all of your weight via burning fat. Lean muscle, fat, and water make up the bulk of your body. This indicates that a person's weight gain or loss might originate from any one of these three sources at any point in time. When you lose weight, you run the danger of losing muscle mass, and the reverse is true when you gain weight. If you don't keep track of your macronutrient intake, you run the danger of losing muscle mass and gaining fat. Maintaining muscle mass while shedding fat and limiting the accumulation of fat in the body may both be achieved by eating a balanced diet high in fat, protein, and carbohydrates.

Improved mood and more energy

Having too little carbs might make you weary and impair your workout performance because carbohydrates are the body's primary energy source. As a result, you are able to ingest the maximum quantity of carbohydrates while effectively burning fat by adjusting your macros correctly. Why not take advantage of the fact that you can eat more and yet lose weight? If you don't have enough fat in your diet, you may have mood swings and other unpleasant side effects as a result. By relying only on "clean" meals, many people find themselves falling short of their daily fat intake. Over a long period of time, under-consumption of fat and/or carbohydrates might make you feel unpleasant. You're already working hard to shed pounds, so there's no need to make things much more difficult.

In the same way that cash is like money, macros are like cash.

Would you rather someone tell you how to spend your money, or would you like to spend it the way you want to. As long as you don't go over your budget, it's okay to spend a lot of money. It is up to you to spend your macros in whatever way you see fit. You may enjoy your favourite meals without sacrificing your fitness goals if you stick to a macronutrient-based diet. It may be easier to maintain a regular lifestyle if you don't follow a strict eating plan that restricts your options. If you find yourself in a situation where you are unable to consume the items in your meal plan, you may be unsure of what to eat. Although someone who knows how many macronutrients they are allowed to eat in any given situation will be more flexible in their food choices. With the help of macronutrients, you may construct a meal plan tailored to your unique needs. It's a no-brainer to stick with your personal macros and eat anything you want.

NO TIME IS WASTED.

Keep an eye on your macronutrient intake to make sure you aren't going too fast or too sluggish in your fitness journey. Trying to shed pounds too quickly might cause muscle loss and exhaustion, but trying to shed pounds slowly can delay noticing improvements in your physical appearance. It is possible to know exactly how much to eat to achieve the weight loss you seek by keeping track of macronutrient consumption. Knowing your macronutrient consumption is especially helpful if you have a specific fitness goal with a set deadline since it helps you stay on track. To put it another way, you have practically complete control over how quickly your body changes. When it comes to fat loss, the "eating clean" approach has been shown to be less successful than macro tracking. Is it possible that even if you follow a "clean" diet, you might reach a weight reduction plateau? No, I don't just eat "cleaner." This method gives you greater control over your weight and enables for precise changes to be made, which in turn helps you to continue progressing towards your goal with the least amount of wasted effort and time possible.

FOOD CONSCIENCE

When you know what macros are, you can make better eating choices. For both short-term and long-term gains, knowing the macronutrient content of the food you consume is essential. For the rest of your days, you will be fueled by food. You may better regulate your body's shape by learning how many calories are in the foods that you eat. To understand why your body looks the way it does, you must be able to compare your daily calorie intake to your body's demands. Instead of making educated guesses about how much food will produce a change in your physique, understanding how many calories your body can tolerate is a far better option.

EASIER THAN YOU EXPECT

While keeping a daily log of your macronutrient intake is helpful, it isn't necessary if you want to make meaningful progress toward your objective. It's a mathematical estimate of how much you should eat to keep on track toward your objective, which is what macronutrient goals are. You can still notice decent effects even if you skip a few grammes of your macros a few days a week. You may only lose 1.9 pounds of fat in a week instead of the expected 2 pounds. Your progress has been made despite the fact that this may not be flawless. If you're familiar with the serving sizes of the foods you regularly consume, it's much easier to keep track of your macronutrient intake this way. Macro tracking may be considered as an everyday meal puzzle. Fitting in all of your favourite meals within your daily macronutrient targets may be a lot of fun.

OPTIMAL

Even if you don't keep track of your macros, you may still build a terrific physique, but the outcomes will be less than ideal. Keeping tabs on your macros is the difference between hoping and knowing for sure that you'll reach your goal in the most time and cost effective manner possible. It's all about making sure you're getting the correct amount of nutrients in order to keep progressing toward your fitness goal. Tracking macros is proved to be the best technique to improve your body in terms of time, stress, and quality of outcomes.

WHEN SHOULD YOU EAT CARBS?

It is worth the effort to learn which meals contain carbohydrates and when to consume them if you utilise energy in every element of your daily life. When you know how carbohydrates work, you can better manage your energy levels and make better decisions about what you eat throughout the day. Consuming carbohydrates in the morning is one of the best times to do so. Because you've probably been sleeping for the previous few hours and haven't eaten anything, this is a likely scenario for you. Therefore, it is best to eat both simple and complex carbohydrates for both immediate and long-term energy. Carbohydrates are also good before and after a workout. Carbohydrates pre-workout will help you train harder, and carbohydrates post-workout will help you repair your muscles and keep your blood sugar levels stable. Carbohydrates may be consumed at any time of day, but these are the most important times to eat them.

Some people believe that consuming carbohydrates at night may induce weight gain since your body isn't able to metabolise the meal while you are in bed. Despite the fact that this myth has been disproved, it is still a smart plan to eat most of your carbohydrates throughout the day, when you are most likely to use them. As long as you satisfy your daily calorie needs, you can consume carbohydrates at night, even though most individuals are less active in the evening.

Chapter Three

WHAT ARE THE BEST TIMES TO EAT PROTEINS?

Protein intake is best spaced out throughout the course of the day. Individuals can consume an unlimited quantity of protein in a single meal because there is no recommended daily intake limit. As long as one's daily protein needs are being fulfilled, research shows that consuming protein in large doses has the same effect on muscle building and weight reduction as ingesting protein in little portions. To put it another way, it doesn't matter how much protein you eat in a single sitting as long as you meet your daily protein needs. Pre- and post-workout are the best times to ingest protein. Protein and amino acids must always be present in the circulation for this strategy to work. Generally speaking, it is best to divide your daily protein intake throughout each of your meals. For example, if your daily protein need is 150 g, you can consume it in three meals of 50 g each or five meals of 30 g each.

When it comes to meat processing, there are three options: cut, maintain, or bulk.

Depending on how many calories you consume over time, you can achieve varied weight-loss goals depending on whether you're in a cut, a maintenance state, or a bulk. To put it another way, you may alter your body's composition by eating more, less, or the same number of calories as it expels each day. You will maintain your current weight if you eat the same number of calories as your body expends each day. Meal B is sometimes referred to as a calorie-maintenance condition (Meal B). When you ingest too few calories, your body tells you that you're hungry, and when you take too many calories, your body tells you that you're full. In this stage, there is no fat loss, but there can be some muscle gain.

You consume less calories than your body needs to maintain its weight in a cut (caloric deficit). In this scenario, your body is forced to use stored fat as a backup source of energy since it doesn't have enough carbohydrates to meet its energy needs. This results in a reduction in body fat, which makes you appear slimmer. Although this caloric condition can tone your body, muscular development is often at a minimal. A cut is designed to help you reduce weight while preserving your lean muscle. Weight training and a protein-rich diet are the greatest ways to guarantee that you don't lose muscle mass throughout a diet cut. People who want to slim down or get a more defined body should concentrate on staying in shape by cutting calories (Meal A). You consume more calories than your body needs to keep its weight in a bulk (caloric excess). Your body will have more energy to devote to muscle healing thanks to the additional calories you've consumed. A calorie surplus might result in an increase in body fat, even though you grow muscle more quickly. A bulk is designed to maximise muscular mass while minimising body fat. People who want to put on weight should put their efforts towards bulking up (Meal C). Rapid muscular gains can be achieved by novices in weight training as long as adequate protein is supplied and the muscles are suitably stimulated.

Dirty food is better than clean food, according to this comparison

The term "clean" refers to foods that have been minimally processed, are high in vitamins and minerals, and include no added fat or sugar. What we call "dirty" food is one that has been too refined or refined to the point that it lacks essential micronutrients. Categorizing food as "dirty" or "clean," as an informal term used to describe its contents, is a waste of time. You may find a plethora of articles discussing the top ten excellent and terrible foods, however these are only critiques of individual items and do not include the other foods that you consume. To put it another way: You aren't just eating food; you're eating it as part of a diet. Excellent or terrible foods do not exist, but there are good and poor diets. If your overall diet isn't aligned with your fitness goals, excluding certain foods like bread or dairy is of little use. Instead of focusing on whether or not a food is clean or unclean, the most important thing is how much of each nutrient it has that will help you achieve your objective. Among these nutrients are the overall quantity of carbohydrates, fat, and protein in the meal you consume, as well as the amount of vitamins and minerals.

"Those who make the most of the way things turn out get the best results." " John Wooden's quote

CARBOHYDRATES AND MINERALS

Micronutrients, such as vitamins and minerals, are essential to the proper functioning of your body. They boost the immune system, promote development, and aid in the digestion of meals. Biologically, vitamins may be found in all living organisms, as they are organic substances. Soil and water combine to form minerals, which are made up of inorganic components. All vitamins are vital to your health, but only a few minerals are. Each vitamin has a unique role to play in the body's overall wellness. The more micronutrients you consume each day, the more efficient your body will be.

Excess vitamins and minerals are either expelled or stored in fat once you've exceeded your daily requirements. Fat-soluble and water-soluble vitamins are two types of vitamins. Before your body can absorb water-soluble vitamins, they must first dissolve in water. As a result, it's critical to get enough of these nutrients each day, as your body cannot store them. In contrast to water-soluble vitamins, fat-soluble vitamins are kept in the body's cells and are not easily eliminated from the body. Their intake is less frequent than that of water-soluble vitamins, but still needs to be sufficient. A fat-soluble vitamin might be hazardous to your body if you take in too much of it. Supplementing with a multivitamin is a good way to ensure that you get all of the vitamins and minerals you need each day, even if you don't eat enough of them.

FIBER IMPORTANCE

When it comes to food, fibre is the component that our systems are unable to break down or absorb. Insoluble and soluble dietary fibres are the two main types. Fruit, vegetables, oats, beans, peas, lentils, and barley all contain soluble fibre. Blood sugar and cholesterol can be controlled and reduced by mixing it with a drink. Fruits, grains, and vegetables all contain insoluble fibre. It functions as a brush to remove waste from the colon. Constipation is less likely when fibre is present in the diet. Diets high in fibre can lower the risk of heart disease, type-2 diabetes, and a number of cancers. Cholesterol, blood pressure, and digestion all improve as well, and you also get a boost in satiety. If you eat too much fibre, you may have bloating or frequent bowel motions. To maintain a healthy heart, the American Heart Association suggests consuming

25 to 38 grammes of fibre daily. Another way to get 10-15 grammes of fibre per 1000 calories is to eat a lot of fruits and vegetables.

HYDRATION

Water is one of the most crucial things you can do to ensure that your body is able to work properly. Every cell in your body needs water to function properly. Hydration is essential for a healthy fluid balance in the body. A few of the many roles performed by these biological fluids include the absorption of nutrients, digestion, blood circulation, saliva production, and temperature regulation. Drinking enough water will help you feel full and reduce the need for a second trip to the grocery store for extra food. A minimum of half a gallon (8 cups) of water per day is advised, with more water needed based on physical activity, health, and weather. To get the most out of your workout, make sure you drink enough of water before, during, and after it. Dizziness, headaches, muscular cramps and dry mouth are all indicators that you need to up your water consumption. A couple glasses of water might sometimes be all you need when you're feeling sluggish, weary, or just "off" today.

Chapter Four

PRECISELY HOW TO READ A NUTRITION FACTS LABEL

You may learn about the contents of a food or beverage by reading the nutrition data label on the packaging. In addition to the item's macronutrient and micronutrient breakdown, the label provides information about the product's ingredients.

If you know what information you're looking for, reading a nutritional label may be a breeze. You're primarily concerned with the total fat, total carbs, and total protein in each portion when it comes to macros. As you can see, the breakdown of calories into these three macronutrients. The serving size listed at the top of the nutrition label corresponds to the number of nutrients and calories you'll see on the label. For the same serving size, a more precise measurement is indicated in the parentheses. For example, you may measure the serving size on this nutrition label by either '1/4 cup' or '113 grammes'.

The'servings per container' tells you how many servings there are in the overall product. A serving size of 8 is included in the container in this situation. The daily proportion of vitamins and minerals in a single serving is shown at the bottom of the label. Aside from the quantity of fibre and salt in a food, additional information might be beneficial.

Tracking fat, protein, and carbohydrate intake is a good way to keep tabs on calories as well. Calorie content per gramme of the following macronutrient sources:

9 calories in a gramme of fat

4 calories for every 1g of carbohydrates

4 calories = 1g of protein per gramme.

You can figure out how many calories you consume by figuring out how many grammes of each macronutrient you consume. The amount of calories in one gramme of each macronutrient is equal to the number of grammes in one gramme of that macronutrient. The total number of calories is then calculated by adding the calories from the three macronutrients. As an illustration, consider the following nutrition label:

2g x 9 = 18 calories of fat per serving

calories from carbs: 16 from 4 grammes

64 calories from protein, which is equal to 16 grammes.

It's 16 + 64 + 18 calories, or 98.

In fact, the 98 calories estimated is quite near to the 100 calories on the label. As a result of rounding, converting grammes to calories may not always be accurate.

You'll always strike the target if you shoot for nothing. He was known as "Zig."

FOOD TRACING

Keeping track of what you consume has never been easier. Using applications like 'MyFitnessPal,' you may search for and monitor any food you come across. You only need to enter the food's name and the amount you want, and you're done. Using a barcode scanner makes it even easier to find exactly what you're looking for. The portion size and the number of servings that you consume may be set once you've selected the meal that you want. Time to do all of this may be spent sending a quick SMS. You may save complete meals in the app so that the next time you consume the same item, it'll be included in your daily food diary in a matter of seconds, making tracking your diet even easier.

Any item you haven't cooked yourself or that doesn't have a nutrition label could be difficult to keep track of. Estimating the amount of each individual component is the best approach to do so. Some examples are two slices of bread, two slices of turkey and cheese, mayonnaise and lettuce on a sandwich cooked by someone else. Even while the purpose of macro monitoring is to be as accurate as possible, in most circumstances it doesn't necessarily have to be. As long as your daily macronutrient targets are within a respectable range, you'll be well on your way to achieving your objective. Your macros will be more accurate since you know precisely how much of the components are in the food you eat when you prepare it yourself.

A person may easily gain or lose weight by using calorie-tracking applications and websites, which are available in plenty. One of the most popular free applications on the market is 'MyFitnessPal,' because to its extensive dietary database and ease of use. With these services at your disposal, it is possible to make informed dietary decisions that help you get closer to your objective. 'Total fat, total carbs, and protein' are important metrics to pay attention to when using 'MyFitnessPal.' When you look at your daily intake, it is summarised in the 'total' column. Knowing how much of each macronutrient you have left might help you pick foods that will help you meet your daily calorie and macronutrient targets.

SUPPLEMENTS

In the majority of cases, people who want to lose weight or build muscle quickly resort to supplements. The purpose of supplements is to "supply" your diet, not to assist you achieve your goals. Most common vitamins may be found in food, but keeping a few on hand is convenient. Here are some suggestions for nutritional supplements to help you achieve your fitness goals.

THE PROTEIN FOUND IN MILK

The powdered version of whey protein is a liquid byproduct of cheese making that is offered as a supplement. With its quick absorption and simple digestion, it has earned the title of "complete protein." With a biological value of 100, whey protein has the greatest possible absorption value as an absorption measurement. Whey protein is an excellent post-workout supplement since it is quickly digested. Additionally, whey protein is handy to use when food is scarce. Smoothies, oats, and other dishes can all benefit from the addition of the powder. Whey protein supplements can help you remain on track with your diet because most individuals find it difficult to get enough protein from their diet alone.

CREATINE

High intensity exercise can be improved by supplementing with creatine, which helps the muscles seem larger. ATP, the energy system responsible for brief bursts of performance, uses creatine as a fuel source. This increases the number of repetitions a person can perform by strengthening the contraction of muscle fibres. This nutrient may be present in animal products including meat, fish, and the human body. The most basic form of creatine molecule, micronized creatine monohydrate, is suggested despite the abundance of creatine mixes available on the market. Creatine monohydrate that has been finely ground into a powder form is known as micronized. Creatine monohydrate should be taken at the recommended dosage of 5 grammes per day. Your body has a limit on how much it can take in, so any surplus will likely be expelled rather than utilised. Water retention in the muscles is caused by this natural chemical, which gives the impression of more defined muscles. On the medical front as well as in sporting contexts, creatine is a well-researched nutrient. Aside from helping you exercise harder and build bigger muscles, creatine can also help you look better.

MULTIVITAMIN

A vast range of vitamins and minerals are needed by the human body to perform its everyday functions. When you're active, your body need extra nutrients to keep up with the demands of your lifestyle. A lack of these micronutrients can have an adverse effect on the efficiency of your body's systems, particularly while you're working out. As a consequence, getting enough vitamins and minerals into your system is critical if you want to achieve your goals. Even if you can obtain all of your micronutrients only through food, it might be difficult to do so on a daily basis. A multivitamin supplement might serve as an insurance policy in the event that you don't acquire enough vitamins and minerals from your diet.

OIL OF THE FISH

A wide range of health advantages have been linked to the essential fatty acids (EFAs) found in fish oil, including improved brain function and cardiovascular and joint health. Omega-3 fatty acids EPA and DHA are two of the most studied and commonly used fatty acids, and they are considered "essential" since our systems cannot make them on their own. As a result, we must eat or take supplements to receive these nutrients. Triglyceride synthesis is reduced by omega-3 fatty acids. Stroke, heart disease, and coronary artery disease can all be brought on by high triglyceride levels. A number of benefits of fish oil have been documented in research, including a boost to the immune system and anti-inflammatory therapy; enhancements to eyesight, cognition and bone health. It's a good investment to eat fish oil because of the numerous health benefits it has to offer.

PRE-WORKOUT

There is no need to use pre-workout vitamins. Beta-alanine, caffeine, creatine, B vitamins, and other performance-enhancing chemicals are common in pre-workout supplements. In addition to increasing endurance, a pre-workout supplement can boost energy, improve attention, and increase blood flow to muscles. When you're feeling lethargic and in need of a pick-me-up to get you through your workout, taking a pre-workout supplement might assist. Taking pre-workout pills before an exercise typically takes between 15 and 30 minutes for the effects to set in. Caffeine is a popular pre-workout supplement alternative since it has been proved to improve training performance on its own.

Nutrient Priority PyraMID

The objective of this pyramid is to eliminate any ambiguity regarding the many facets of nutrition that should be taken into account when working toward a fitness goal. The most critical priority is at the bottom of the pyramid, and it ascends in significance from there. It aims to change your body's composition by either increasing muscle mass or decreasing fat mass. Most people who are preparing for a certain goal have no notion what their dietary priorities should be. The nuances of a person's objective might get in the way of focusing on the most important aspects of nutrition that will help them achieve their desired outcome. If you don't know what to look for, you can ask, "Should I drink 2 percent milk or whole milk?" and get an incorrect response. The person's fitness goals, macronutrient needs, and other considerations must be taken into account before offering a valid response. If you're unsure about what foods should take precedence in your diet, consult this pyramid for guidance. Eric Helms, a coach at '3DMuscleJourney,' came up with the idea for this pyramid.

WELL-BEING OF THE ENERGY

Rebuilding your physique requires a careful balance between the calories you take in and the calories your body expends (physical activity). In the end, your weight fluctuation is determined by these two variables. Depending on how you balance your calorie intake, you can gain, reduce, or maintain your ideal body weight. You'll maintain your current weight if the number of calories you take in and the number of calories you expend are equal. You will acquire weight if your daily caloric intake exceeds your daily caloric expenditure. Finally, reducing weight is a result of consuming less calories than you expend each day.

It's important to know the quantity of calories you require in order to reach your specific objective before determining your caloric balance (energy balance). To figure out how many calories you need to maintain your current weight, it's typical to begin by figuring out how many calories your body needs to function. Age, height, weight, gender, and degree of physical activity all have a role in determining calorie needs. The quantity of calories your body needs to maintain its present weight may be estimated using these criteria (the actual amount of calories you require is determined by how your body metabolises the food you consume). Once you know how many calories you need to maintain your current weight, you may either cut or raise the quantity of calories you consume to achieve your desired weight. The rate at which you lose or gain weight will be determined by the number of calories you cut or add. While in a caloric deficit, the pace at which your weight fluctuates may effect how much muscle mass you retain and how much fat you acquire.

It's difficult to maintain a healthy energy balance if you don't know how many calories you're consuming. To avoid disappointment, make sure your energy levels are in balance before embarking on a new exercise programme. When trying to alter your body's composition, the first step is to determine if you are in a deficit, excess, or at maintenance calorie intake.

Two. Micronutrients.

Knowing where the calories in your diet come from will help you maintain a healthy weight. There are three macronutrients that make up a calorie: lipids (fat), protein (protein), and carbohydrates. Knowing how much of these macronutrients we take in our diet is useful. For example, a person's diet may consist of 40% protein, 40% carbohydrates, and 20% fat. Instead of using percentages, the grammes of macronutrients can be measured. The way the body changes and how it feels will be affected by the different dimensions. Even if you eat the same number of calories, changing the balance of macronutrients in your diet can alter your body's structure. If you want to lose weight, you should up your protein intake while lowering your carbohydrate intake, and vice versa if you want to put on weight, you should do the opposite. In order to achieve a certain goal, it may be useful to work with an expert coach who can help you tailor your diet to your individual needs. In the 'Why Track Macros' section, you'll find more information on macronutrients and how they effect your body.

Water and micronutrients

Micronutrients are equally as crucial as macronutrients when it comes to your body's composition, if not more so. A lack of vitamins and minerals might have an impact on your fitness progress. Maintaining a healthy body and supporting the metabolism of lipids, protein, and carbohydrates are the primary functions of micronutrients. Fruits and vegetables are rich sources of vitamins and minerals. At least one serving of fruits and vegetables should be consumed for every 1000 calories consumed. A person who eats 2000 calories per day should eat at least two servings of fruits and at least two dishes of vegetables. Getting adequate vitamins and minerals is easier if you eat a wide variety of complete foods. Vitamins and minerals are covered in further detail in the 'Vitamins and Minerals' section of this article.

Consuming enough amounts of water is critical to achieving any type of fitness goal. Inadequate hydration may have a negative impact on the way your body feels and functions since water is involved in every biological function. You can tell if you're drinking enough water by the number of clear urinations you have during the day. Drinking extra water when working toward a fitness goal isn't something that has to be watched as strictly as the previous two stages because most individuals don't have a problem with it. There is additional information on the significance of drinking water in the 'Hydration' part of the website.

MEAL TIMING AND REGULARITY

However, if executed correctly, meal timing and frequency can have a positive impact on fat reduction and muscle building. Changes in your body composition are ultimately determined by your caloric and macronutrient makeup. The advantages of eating at specific times of the day are more focused on how you feel and how much energy you have when training. Carbohydrates should be consumed 1-2 hours before to working out in order to ensure that you have enough energy to train, even if some people do well without doing so.

It's more of a personal preference than a necessity to eat at precise times in order to lose weight or develop muscle. To maximise fat loss and muscle gain, eating three to five times a day is ideal, but it isn't necessary as long as the daily caloric needs are satisfied. Spreading out your protein intake throughout the day is the greatest way to optimise the potential advantages of developing muscle. Consuming protein and carbohydrates immediately after an exercise has been demonstrated to aid in muscle repair. It's a good idea to keep glucose control and hunger levels in mind when deciding when to eat. Carbohydrates are best consumed in the morning, immediately following an exercise, and towards the end of the day. "Eat when you're hungry" is a basic rule of thumb when it comes to meal frequency. The '6 Meals a Day' section of 'Common Misconceptions' explains more about meal time and frequency.

Five. ADDITIONAL SERVICES.

This is the lowest rung on the priority ladder. To supplement what you don't receive naturally from your diet, you should take supplements Using the name "supplement" itself indicates that it is meant to fill in the gaps in your diet. Supplementing with whey protein, for example, may make sense for someone who struggles to receive all of their protein intake from their diet alone. Supplements aren't a substitute for real food when it comes to getting the nourishment you need. Here's where most people go astray because they mistakenly believe that relying solely on dietary supplements to achieve their goals is a viable option. These people may not succeed since they haven't paid attention to the most vital components of their diet. Checking reviews and doing your own research might help you determine if a supplement will have a substantial influence on your desired outcomes when purchasing one of these products. Pay attention to the product's quality and how beneficial it would be for you if you're pursuing a certain objective. In the 'Supplements' area, you'll learn which supplements are best for accomplishing various outcomes.

LIFESTYLE AND CONDUCT

However, this subject isn't only a stage in the pyramid and should be taken into account at all levels. While focusing on your diet and exercise, remember that your objective should be attainable and not take over your life. Some people give up on their diets early because they don't love the restrictions and feel deprived. Some people, on the other hand, are perfectionists who strive to reach perfection in all they do. Remember that being cheerful, optimistic, and having a good time is an important component of being fit. Everyone should be able to eat what they want because there is such a vast range of food available across the world. Allowing yourself the freedom to eat the foods you enjoy helps you stay on track with your diet. Over the course of a lifetime, it's impossible to eat a diet that restricts you while denying yourself the things you enjoy. MyFitnessPal and other calorie-aware apps like it allow you to effortlessly search the nutritional content of practically any item you can think of.

To achieve fantastic results, you don't have to worry about achieving your daily calorie or macro goals. Your body's daily quota of nutrients may be a powerful tool for you to use when it comes to deciding how much food or drink you consume. Despite the occasional setbacks, if you stick to your diet, you'll get the results you're looking for. Despite the importance of resisting temptation and being as consistent as possible, you should not allow yourself to be consumed by the effort. Maintaining a healthy lifestyle while pursuing any type of fitness goal is essential.

PREMIUM FORMATION

Most individuals miss opportunities because they appear to be hard labour. courtesy of Ann Landers

Groups of muscles

The chest, back, shoulders, legs, biceps, triceps, and abdominal muscles are among the many muscular groups that make up the human body. Leg workouts often target the quadriceps, hamstrings, and calves, as well as the glutes. It is the upper traps and deltoids that make up the shoulder blades (delts). The front, lateral, and rear delts are the three primary muscles of the deltoid. The name "biceps" refers to the two main heads of the biceps; the term "triceps" refers to the three primary heads of the triceps. The lats, upper, middle, and lower backs are all part of the back. When doing particular workouts, certain muscle groups function in concert. For example, the chest is the primary target of the flat bench press, but the triceps and shoulders also play an important role in its execution. Your workout will be more effective when you know which muscles are being targeted by the movements you're doing.

WHEN AND HOW DO MUSCLE TISSUES EXPAND?

When you lift weights, you cause muscular injury. Pumping iron in the gym actually depletes your body of muscle-building nutrients and causes small rips in your muscle fibres, which may seem bizarre. After your workout, your body begins to repair the damage you imposed on it, and you begin to see the muscular growth you seek. 3. Soreness is typically a result of muscle fibres bleeding and ripping after an ineffective workout. Muscles mend and get stronger when they are damaged, which is a sign that you're growing muscle. For optimal muscle growth, 48 hours of rest is required every two days.

It's called progressive overload, and it's the driving force behind muscular growth. In order to get the most out of your muscles, you need to put more strain on them than they are used to. Your muscles develop larger and stronger as a biological response to this stress. Progressive overload, such as increasing the weight or the number of reps, is required for further muscular growth once your muscles have adapted to the stress by getting stronger. Muscles are damaged during exercise, and they recover and develop while you are at rest.

"Progress is impossible without hardship." Douglass, Frederick

Chapter Five

HOW TO DECIDE ON A WORKOUT

You may create a strong foundation of muscle by adhering to simple exercises. Compound exercises like the squat, bench press, and deadlift work more muscle groups while burning more calories than single-joint exercises. In order to target a single muscle, isolation exercises such as the bicep curl or leg extension are used. Compound workouts and isolation exercises can both be beneficial to your training regimen. To work every part of the muscle group, a variety of exercises should be performed. You may build a more detailed and defined physique by performing efficient exercises that target different angles on the muscle.

HOW TO BECOME WARM

Three phases are required for a complete warm-up. The first step is to increase your core body temperature in preparation for the level of exertion that is about to come your way. Jogging, riding or doing jumping jacks for 5 to 10 minutes should be enough cardiac activity to get the job done. Stretching and strengthening your muscles and joints is the second step. Stretching for an additional 5-10 minutes will assist your muscles be more resistant and less prone to injury. In certain cases, but not always, a complete body stretch is beneficial. To be mobile is to be able to move around without restriction. Preventing injuries and maximising range of motion during exercising are both made possible through mobility exercises. Finally, you should begin your workout with small weights in order to prepare your muscles for weight training.

Starting an exercise with light weights allows you to get a better sense of the action and prepares your muscles for higher loads. As a result of not warming up properly, your performance will be hindered, and you will be more likely to suffer from post-workout soreness.

ABOUT HOW MUCH WEIGHT ARE WE TALKING?

It's important to pick a weight that's appropriate for the number of reps you're planning on doing without compromising on technique. To avoid pain and ineffective outcomes, most people choose a weight that is excessively heavy and end up with poor form. It might be difficult to induce muscular development if the weight used is too low. To summarise, decide on a desired rep range and then select a weight that will push you to your physical limits for the specified number of reps. Use a small weight while starting a new workout until you get the hang of the proper technique. Gradually raise the weight until the needed number of repetitions is tough once you have mastered the form. You'll ultimately need to raise the weight as you become stronger and can do more repetitions at this weight. It's not always a good idea to perform an exercise with the heaviest weight possible. You may only be able to finish one or two repetitions of an exercise, but if you choose a smaller weight that allows you to complete more repetitions, you'll see more muscle growth.

WHERE ARE THE REPS AND SETS?

A single exercise performance is referred to as a "repetition." The number of repetitions in a set of ten bicep curls is equal to the number of sets. To a large extent, your training approach is dictated by the number of repetitions that you perform. For example, you can exercise for physical endurance, strength, or a mixture of the two. Muscular endurance training benefits from high repetitions (12-20), whilst strength training benefits from low repetitions (3-8). At an appropriate range of 8-12 repetitions, you may train your muscles for both strength and endurance. Adjusting the weight may be necessary on a regular basis. While training for strength and endurance, the weight may be too heavy if you can't complete eight repetitions. Generally speaking, you should not be able to complete 12 repetitions with the weight you are using. You'll ultimately discover a weight that pushes you to your limits inside that rep range through trial and error.

In order to train till failure, you must finish all of the repetitions with proper form. At this stage in a workout, proper form must be sacrificed for the sake of one more repetition. Muscles can grow even if you don't push yourself to the point of exhaustion. For the majority of your sets, aim to complete the exercise with 1-2 reps remaining before failing. Working your muscles to exhaustion is something that should only be done at the finish of a workout or session. However, despite the fact that training to failure should be utilised very seldom, you don't have to limit your sets to a certain number of repetitions. In the event that you are able to execute 1-2 extra reps with good form after completing your goal number of reps in a set, do so. You'll know if you've stimulated muscle development or not after the final few reps.

Reps performed in the same manner over the course of several sets are referred to as sets. You should perform at least one warm-up set with a lesser weight for each exercise before progressing to higher weights. A normal number of sets per exercise is between three and five, however no exact number of sets should be followed. The more sets you do, the more likely it is that your muscles will expand. A reasonable number of sets each exercise allows for more time and energy to be spent on other activities.

PERIOD OF REST IN BETWEEN SETTINGS

The quality and intensity of your training are strongly influenced by the quantity of rest you take in between sets. It's common for people to procrastinate starting their next set, which reduces the effectiveness of their workout. The muscle pumps blood after completing one set of a particular activity. Gaining new muscle mass is much easier when you have a good temporary pump. Your chances of getting rid of this pump increase with each passing minute that passes without starting the following set. If you don't take enough time to recover between sets, your workout will be less effective since your muscles will become fatigued faster. You want to allow your muscles some time to rest, but keep the rest period short enough to keep your body guessing about how well it can function. Depending on your goals, you may need more or less relaxation time. The rest time in between sets may be used to target each of these training types, despite the fact that they are interdependent. Rest intervals of 3-5 minutes are advised for strength training, 1-2 minutes for muscular growth, and 45-90 seconds for endurance training, according to the American Council on Exercise. Compound workouts, which employ several muscle groups, can be more demanding and require more recuperation than single-muscle exercises. In addition, the amount of time spent sleeping varies from person to person. An individual can recuperate after a working set in 30 seconds, whereas another may require 60 seconds. To get the best outcomes, you need to strike a balance between getting enough sleep and getting too little.

TOTAL TRAINING SCHEDULE

Sets, reps, and weight are all factors that contribute to the total volume of training. The overall volume is affected by each of these elements. Regardless of how heavy or light you choose to exercise, you can always attain the same volume of training by adjusting the sets, weights, or reps you perform. There's no difference in the total number of repetitions between a 50lb and 100lb weight when it comes to doing a 20-rep set. As seen, you can tailor your exercise to your preferred training approach by varying the number of reps, weight, and sets while still maintaining complete control over the volume. Volume serves as a measure of how much effort is put into an exercise, while other elements such as rest periods between sets will influence intensity.

APPROPRIATE FORMULA

In order to achieve the body you desire, it is critical to perform a workout correctly. Proper form helps you to use your muscles to their greatest potential while also reducing the chance of damage. Some people cheat appropriate form and momentum in order to lift huge weights. Use a weight that permits you to do the exercise correctly rather than sacrificing form for the sake of a larger weight. How much damage you can inflict on the muscle is the key to growing muscle, not how much weight you can lift. The mind-muscle link improves when good form is used during the workout. Connecting an activity to a specific muscle contraction helps to keep it engaged throughout the movement. The more you can manage the weight with your muscles, the more progress you can make. Progress in your training is shown by an increase in the usage of good form. Consequently, learning the proper technique for a workout is essential for increasing muscular mass and strength.

INDICATES THAT YOUR TRAINING IS WORKING

Lifting larger weights is typically considered as the only indicator of progress in training. There are several more indicators that you've progressed in your training, such as being able to lift greater weight. The capacity to perform more reps with less rest, as well as an increase in form, are all markers of progress. The ability to perform an additional rep with the same weight from last week to this week is a clear indication of improvement in your squats, for example. So what if increasing the weight or repetitions doesn't result in progress? By reducing the time between sets, you give your muscles less time to recuperate, increasing the difficulty of the workout. Increasing your training efficiency means that you can finish the same set of exercises with less time spent resting.

The capacity to do an exercise with perfect form is an indicator of progress that is often neglected. Your muscles are challenged just as much by maintaining proper technique as they are by adding weight or completing more repetitions. Another measure of development in your training is doing the same workout with improved form. Your progress will be more evident if you stick to a regular workout schedule. It will take some time before you observe substantial changes in your body's health. Although you may not notice much improvement for a few weeks, you will ultimately get the results you have been training for if you have patience, persistence, and hard effort. Muscle, strength, endurance, or mental toughness can all contribute to training progress. It doesn't matter what type of progress you make, you'll get closer to accomplishing your fitness goal with each one.

"Look not at what a person has actually accomplished, but at what he desires to do" According to Khalil Gibran

CONTROLLED RESPIRATORY SYSTEM

The brain, spinal cord, and a vast network of neurons make up the central nervous system. Sending, receiving, and interpreting information is the primary function of this system, which may be found all over the body. Maintaining the health of your central nervous system (CNS) is critical since it governs every thought and action in your body. The central nervous system (CNS) can be harmed by too much training and not enough recovery time. It is impossible to replace or repair most of the cells in your central nervous system. Injuries can cause physical and cognitive difficulties, as well as other symptoms. The CNS is more vulnerable to harm while ingesting fewer calories than usual, highlighting the need of getting enough nutrients and resting when on a diet. It's possible to overwork your CNS, just like your muscles. You can, however, safeguard and maintain the health of your central nervous system with adequate diet and efficient training.

A DAY OF REST.

Taking a full day off from training every now and then is essential for your body's recuperation. Increased exercise frequency puts your muscles, tendons, ligaments, bones, and joints under additional stress, increasing your chance of injury. When you lift weights, your muscles are torn down, therefore your body needs time to heal itself and generate new muscle fibres. It may be a good idea to focus on one muscle group at a time so that other muscles have a chance to recuperate. It is possible to exercise one muscle group while recovering another by doing upper and lower body workouts on separate days. Taking a rest day can increase training performance, boost your immune system, and give you more stamina and energy. Even on a rest day, you may stay in shape with a little running, yoga, or stretching.

IS THERE A PERFECT RATE FOR TRAINING?

The number of days per week you train should be determined by the amount of effort you put in and your level of physical fitness. How much stress you put on your body is mostly determined by the intensity of your workout. Because of this, it is possible to exercise more frequently when exercising with moderate effort rather than when training with high intensity. The frequency of training is also influenced by a person's physical capabilities. Training at a high intensity 6-7 days a week may be OK for an athlete, but someone who is just starting out in the gym should only do so 3-4 days a week. Working out should be manageable and in line with your fitness goals.

Individuals should plan their workouts around their own recovery times. Knowing how your body responds to training might help you schedule your exercises more effectively since different muscles recover at different rates. Allow at least 48 hours for muscles to recuperate following a workout before exercising the same set of muscles again. Before you can train the same muscle group again, you must give it adequate rest and nourishment. If you're still hurting after your last workout, you're probably not ready to exercise that particular body area again. Protecting the health of one's central nervous system is equally important. A person's central nervous system (CNS) might be harmed even if they have the stamina to workout at a high level daily. It's important to keep an eye on your general health while deciding how often to work out, as there are many variables to consider.

Chapter Six

IO COMMON MISTAKES IN TRAINING

TOO MUCH WEIGHT IN THE LIFT

It's not always beneficial to use greater weight to get a better exercise. You may gain more muscle if you let go of your ego. Using too much weight may need poor form in order to complete the exercise, thus it is essential to activate the muscle as much as feasible. It's preferable to start with a weight that's manageable for the duration of the activity and then work your way up to something more challenging.

BAD TECHNIQUES 2.

Bad form prevents some people from reaping the benefits of their exercise. It is possible to execute 20 "bicep curls" yet hardly work your muscle due of poor technique. Your workouts will be more fruitful if you use simple tactics like eliminating momentum and controlling the weight with your target muscle. It is also less likely that you will be injured if you use the proper form.

If you haven't done your homework before going to the gym, you'll be under-prepared.

Watching others work out at the gym might help some people figure out what to do themselves. To maximise your success and save time, avoid starting an exercise without a strategy in place beforehand. Researching routines, appropriate exercise techniques, and general training advice may help you become more effective and adaptable in your training. Check out my "Resources to Maximize Your Fitness Potential" area for online fitness guidance.

EXPECTATIONS THAT ARE UNREALISTIC

The idea that you may acquire your ideal body in a matter of days is naive. As time goes on, your body will adapt. Getting the body you want may take weeks or even months, depending on your present health and fitness level. Be patient and focus on one day at a time, and you'll get there eventually.

Chapter Seven

THINGS TO DO TO MAKE IT WORK

Remaining in the same position for too long

Everyone needs a break in between sets, but most people take much too long. As a result, they wind up texting or conversing too much, which allows their bodies to become excessively relaxed. Resting too long might have a detrimental effect on your training. To push your body, shorten the rest periods between sets.

6. Doubting Yourself.

Negative thoughts might have a negative impact on your training. Maintaining a happy attitude is key to getting the most out of your workout. Remember that everytime you do anything new, you have no option but to make progress.. Keep your eyes on the prize and have faith that you can achieve it.

Doing too much at one time

Many other components of fitness may be improved, including cardiovascular exercise, weight training, a balanced diet, drinking more water, planning your meals, and obtaining more sleep. Most people find it difficult to do everything at once. Instead of making a large change at once, it's best to take modest steps toward your fitness objective.

EATING TOO FEW CALORIES.

Starting a healthy diet is a wonderful way to become fit and minimise the calorie content of a meal plan. Consuming too little calories, along with excessive exercise, might make one feel lethargic. If you're trying to lose weight, it's crucial to make sure you're getting enough calories in your diet to keep you going throughout the day. You can consume as many calories as possible while still meeting your weight loss goals if your macronutrients are set up correctly.

INABILITY TO FIND DIFFERENT EXERCISES

A well-rounded body can only be achieved with a varied training regimen. Exercises become more efficient if you know which muscles are being used in each one. Because the muscles in your legs are made up of several distinct groups, it's a good idea to do exercises that work on all of them.

10. FAILURE TO WARM UP

It's critical to properly prepare your body before beginning a workout so that it can handle the stress of training effectively. Preventing injury and enhancing training performance are two of the main benefits of warming up before a workout.

MENTAL FITNESS TRAINING

Focus. This is the primary distinction between working out and training. Workout consists of completing activities without a specific purpose in mind. "Training" necessitates that you engage in physical activity while also strengthening your mental fortitude. It's your mindset that separates you from those who merely want to workout for the sake of training. A person who trains pushes through each and every set, even if they feel like they're burning out. Fighting through a set is painful, but the strength you get from it lasts a lifetime. To improve your self-discipline, focus on your workout and keep it up for as long as possible.

With a strategy in place, a person who intends to work out arrives at the gym with no worries about what to do when they there. It's best to map out your workout ahead of time so that you can concentrate only on getting the job done and nothing else. It's better to have a terrible plan than no strategy at all. Anyone who comes to the gym to work out isn't concerned about the other people there. If you see someone else watching you train, don't be ashamed. If anybody should be humiliated, it should be the one who is observing since they should also be training. To get the most out of your workout, you should concentrate on getting the most out of each activity.

Make it a goal to outperform your last workout. As a result of your mental condition, you will either be able to lift more weight or do more repetitions throughout a workout. If you want a better physique, you must psychologically drive yourself through your workouts. Instead of waiting for your muscles to expand, push yourself to the maximum and watch them do so. In order to achieve your fitness objective, think of each session as increasing your strength by one percent. Strengthening your training attitude will help you improve other areas of your life, such as your self-confidence. Most individuals only notice the physical benefits of working out, but real progress in your physical appearance begins with a shift in your mental attitude toward the process.

THEORY OF OPTIMAL FITNESS

"Learning to dance in the rain is more important than waiting for the storm to pass." In the words of Greg Plitt

COMMON FACTS ABOUT FITNESS

It's easy to get caught up in the hype of many fitness ideas that promise to be able to assist you in achieving your objectives. Some can help you, while others can lead you down a path that requires more work than is required and yields results that are deceptive. This section aims to dispel some of the most common myths about how to get the body of your dreams.

CARDIO TO LOSE WEIGHT IS A MISTAKE, TO SAY THE LEAST.

Many people attempt to shed pounds by logging countless hours on the treadmill. Cardio exercise is beneficial to overall health, but it isn't required if you want to lose weight. Cardio workouts like jogging, biking, and using an elliptical machine can all help you lose weight, but your body's calorie balance is what ultimately determines whether or not you lose weight. As long as your nutrition isn't in order, cardio might be useless. A person might gain weight even if they exercise 10 miles and expend 1,000 calories, but then eat 1,500 calories of food afterward. Controlling your food is the most effective way to lose weight. Running a mile burns about the same amount of calories as a banana. So, would it be better to run a mile or simply not eat a banana? It's probably simpler to avoid jogging a mile if you're not a monkey with banana fantasies. This is a great illustration of how you may achieve your objective more efficiently rather than pushing yourself to death.

Cardio can help you burn more calories after your diet is in order. Even though exercise helps you lose weight, overdoing it might leave you with a flat appearance in your muscles. On the other side, weight training focuses on developing your muscles, which enhances the overall look of your body. Don't waste your calories on activities that won't produce the outcomes you desire. A well-defined physique can be achieved without the use of cardio, although this isn't always the case. With a low-calorie diet, it might be difficult to get your body the nutrients it needs. As a result, exercise can help you burn more calories and prevent having to cut back on your caloric intake in order to lose weight.

Toning is a common misconception.

A "toned" appearance that most people seek can only be achieved by reducing body fat or increasing muscle. You'll be able to further define your body if you combine the two methods. Fat accumulation and fat loss can only be accomplished through the manipulation of your muscles. Fat cannot be converted into muscle, and muscle cannot be converted into fat. In order to lose weight, you must expend more energy than you take in. Muscle growth is only possible when you put your muscles under a sufficient amount of stress to cause them to expand. Some people want to maintain their current weight while having a sculpted figure. Since the density of muscle is greater than that of fat, it is possible to maintain the same weight while achieving a more aesthetically pleasing appearance. Muscles require a long time to build, however fat loss occurs very quickly. With these effects in a short amount of time, your weight is likely to drop as a result of fat loss.

MISTAKE #3: SEEKING TO LOSE WEIGHT INSTEAD OF FAT

Individuals who are looking to reduce weight in certain areas of their body may opt for a specialised diet or exercise regimen. It is impossible to reduce fat in a specific area of your body. Your DNA already dictates where you'll gain and lose weight. Depending on where the fat is located on your body, it may take longer to go. For example, a person may shed most of their arm fat while still carrying a significant amount of belly fat. Losing fat from the lower tummy is notoriously tough. You'll have to keep dieting to get rid of the stubborn fat in that place. When the body achieves a lower proportion of body fat, it will eventually opt to burn fat in the resistant locations. In order to burn fat in a specific area of your body, there is no activity or supplement that can do so.

FALSE IDEAS NUMBER FOUR: ABSTRACT TRAINING

There are some who feel that if you want to get a great set of abs, you need to work out every day. Unlike other muscles in your body, your abdominal muscles require time to recuperate, so don't train them every day. Training the abs requires a high number of repetitions and brief rest times between each set. Adding weight to your ab workouts will help you build greater muscle mass. The upper, lower, and oblique portions of your abs should all be included in your training routine. In order to show your abs, you must have a body fat percentage low enough. If you have a thick layer of fat covering your muscles, you won't be able to see them expand.

MISTAKE #5: CONSCIOUSLY INGESTING BAD FOOD

You don't have to sacrifice your health in order to reach your fitness goals. In order to feel less guilty about eating, you need to know more about how your body processes food. Carbohydrates, fats, and proteins may be found in everything you consume. If you consume a cheeseburger and stay within your daily macronutrient objectives, you won't disrupt your fat loss or muscle building efforts.

Many people are misled by the IIFYM (If It Falls Your Macros) weight loss philosophy, which suggests that you may eat whatever you want as long as it fits within your macronutrient targets. While doing so may help you obtain your ideal figure, your overall health will be jeopardised in the process. Make sure you're receiving the majority of your nutrients from whole meals each day before you indulge in a hamburger or milkshake.

ALCOHOL IS THE SECOND MISCONCEPTION

In order to keep their fitness goals on track, many people are frightened to indulge in alcoholic drinks. As long as you limit yourself to one or two drinks, you're OK. If you know how many calories are in a drink and how many calories you're permitted to consume, you can remain on track with your fitness goals. Drinking calories can be replaced with fat or carbohydrate portions that day, but make sure you're receiving enough good nutrients from food because alcohol does not. Increase your calorie expenditure by adding more cardio or physical activity to your daily routine. To avoid dehydration and excessive drinking, it is best to drink a lot of water before the event. A little wine or beer here and there won't hurt your progress as long as you stick to a balanced diet and avoid overindulgence.

FALSE BELIEF #7: Eating too much sugar

True, excessive sugar consumption has long-term health consequences, including diabetes, organ failure, and a variety of ailments. In terms of weight reduction, sugar doesn't matter as long as you're getting the calories you need to burn fat, because it's not going to stop you from losing weight. When carbs are absorbed in your body, they are completely converted into sugar. When it comes to food sources, there are those that break down more slowly like complex carbohydrates and those that break down more quickly like sugar. The more active you are, the more carbohydrates you are permitted to eat since your body uses carbs as its major source of fuel during physical exercise. A higher intake of sugar is not as harmful to those who exercise regularly since their bodies are able to use it instead of storing it.

Because it is so simple to overindulge in sugar, it has a poor reputation. Having too much of something is harmful for you, just like anything else. Whole foods, which are more nutrient dense and satisfying, can aid in lowering one's daily sugar intake. When it comes to fat loss, swapping raw honey or agave nectar for sugar is of little consequence because they still include simple carbohydrates, which your body converts to sugar. However, sugar substitutes with no calories, such as 'Equal,' 'Splenda,' or stevia, will make a difference. In order to stay on track with your fitness goals, it is important to know how much carbohydrates you may ingest.

SODIUM TOO MUCH IS THE 8TH MISTAKE

The amount of salt you consume has a negligible impact on fat loss or muscle gain. This is more of a preventative measure for your overall health than a requirement for enhancing your physical appearance. Lowering blood pressure and reducing the risk of heart disease and stroke can both be achieved by controlling salt intake. In the body, sodium binds to water and maintains a proper fluid balance. When combined with potassium, sodium aids cellular electric activity, which is necessary for a variety of physiological activities such as electrical transmission between nerve fibres, muscle contraction, and others. So restricting your salt consumption without any respect to how much you truly need, might be a possible problem. The body cannot operate without sodium

Because your weight changes during the day due to a rise in salt in the blood, the body retains more water. In order to lose weight, it is necessary to reduce salt consumption, however this is primarily due to the temporary loss of water from the body. For the majority of people's objective of shedding pounds, it's not about losing water but rather burning fat. When preparing for a bodybuild-ing competition or a picture session, it's very crucial to keep an eye on your salt consumption. When they are already thin enough to show the definition of their muscles, bodybuilders and models may choose to increase their salt consumption in order to achieve a dry, skin-tight appearance.

METABOLISM IS THE 9TH MISTAKE.

People frequently blame their slow progress toward fitness on their metabolism. Some people believe that consuming particular meals can increase their metabolism and help them lose weight, while others are sceptical. There is a "grey" region surrounding the concept of metabolism for the majority of people, and it may use some explanation. This is because the term "metabolism" keeps popping up in incorrect beliefs. Metabolic rate refers to how much food your body can digest in a day. It's the process through which your body transforms the food and liquid you consume into usable energy. The number of calories your body needs to operate is determined by your basal metabolic rate (BMR). Your BMR is influenced by a variety of factors, including your weight, gender, and age.

For the most part, your body's energy needs to metabolise meals remain stable and aren't readily altered5. As a result, depending on particular meals to help you burn fat is pointless. It's in your best interest to eat just when your body tells you that you're starving and to stop after you've consumed enough calories to keep your metabolism running smoothly. "Slow" metabolism indicates that your body uses less calories than usual for someone of your size and shape, whereas "rapid" metabolism suggests that you may consume more calories than the average person. If you wish to eat more food without gaining weight because your metabolism is sluggish, you can boost your daily caloric demand by engaging in more physical activity. Whatever your metabolic rate, it's critical to determine how many calories your body requires to maintain its weight and base your exercise goals on that number.

#10: "I'm too fat to gain weight."

There are certain people who have a difficult difficulty gaining weight. "I eat a lot of food, but I don't gain weight" or "I've tried to eat more food, but it doesn't work" are common statements. Eating more will solve the problem. To acquire weight, you must maintain a daily caloric intake higher than your daily caloric expenditure over time. Your body need a certain quantity of calories merely to operate and it needs more when you increase physical activity. This number of calories must be consumed consistently over a period of weeks or months in order to observe a noticeable change in your body. If you're struggling to put on weight, don't give up hope. You just need to discover the proper combination of calories for your metabolism. There is a direct correlation between hunger and fullness in terms of how your body communicates with your brain. A lack of a calorie surplus might result from people eating less when they are full, which is generally the case for most people. For this reason, gaining weight might be a challenge for certain people who do not know how many calories they are eating. If you want to gain weight, you must eat the quantity of calories your body instructs you to eat regardless of whether or not you feel full. If you know what meals are high in calories, you'll be able to eat more without feeling stuffed.

Myth #11: Eating six times a day.

A common myth is that increasing your metabolism by eating five to six little meals a day can help you lose weight. Increasing your metabolism by eating smaller, more frequent meals is a non-issue. The overall number of calories you consume is the most important element in determining whether or not you will lose or gain weight. An average daily caloric intake of 3,000 calories comes from six 500-calorie meals. If you eat three 1,000-calorie meals a day, you'll have a total of 3,000 calories for the day. The consequences are the same whether you consume three meals a day or six. Increasing the number of times you eat each day does not have an immediate effect on your metabolic rate. Changing your body's composition might take days or weeks, thus prioritising the number of meals you eat each day has little effect on fat loss or muscle gain. Even minor things like meal time are unimportant if you don't have the daily total calories you need to achieve your fitness goals on track each day. Before obsessing over the frequency of meals, it's important to understand how much fat, protein, and carbohydrate the body needs. As long as you've met your daily macronutrient requirements, you can eat whenever you want.

BELIEF MISTAKE No. 12: DINNER TIME

Many people are afraid to eat at night when attempting to lose weight. Even when you're sleeping, your body is continuously burning calories to keep itself running and repair damaged tissues. When you get up in the morning, you'll notice that you're lighter than you were the night before since your body is burning more calories. Any time of day that you consume less calories than you expend will result in weight loss, as long as your caloric deficit is greater than your calorie intake. You can effectively lose weight while ingesting the majority of your daily caloric intake at night by following diets like intermittent fasting. Carbohydrate consumption during the day may help with energy levels, but this is a personal preference that has no bearing on fat loss or muscle gain.

No. 13: Eating fat makes you fat.

A high fat diet will not lead you to gain weight if you are not eating more calories than your body requires. A person's weight growth is mostly determined by the ratio of calories consumed and calories expended in the body. This diet allows you to consume a lot of fat and little carbohydrate while still losing weight thanks to the Ketogenic diet. Despite this, it is possible for someone to eat very little fat while consuming a lot of calories, and their body will still store the excess calories as fat. In comparison, one gramme of fat provides 9 calories, whereas one gramme of carbs or protein provides just 4 calories per serving. Fat provides around two and a half times as many calories per gramme as the other two macronutrients combined. So, limiting fat consumption isn't because it's unhealthy for you; rather, it's due to fat's high calorie content. An individual's fat consumption should be based on his or her own personal needs. The idea is to preserve a healthy level of fat in your system while still making progress toward your fitness objectives.

EXERCISING TOO MUCH IS A MISTAKE, NOT A TREAT

When people learn about the numerous advantages of regular physical activity, they are more likely to want to continue doing so. You may train as often as you like if you follow a healthy diet, exercise, and rest schedule. An individual's level of intensity, volume, recuperation, and caloric intake all play a role in determining how often they should exercise. Overtraining occurs when your training has a negative impact on other parts of your health, such as your cardiovascular health. If you're experiencing any of these symptoms, it's possible that you've reached the point of overtraining. Overworking your central nervous system is a common cause of these symptoms. To avoid overtraining, it is essential to know when to give oneself a full day of relaxation. As long as you supply your body with adequate nutrients and recuperation time, you may train as often as you like.

Exercising in the wrong way might lead to musculoskeletal problems.

You may have heard that in order to prevent your muscles from becoming used to your workouts, you need switch up your exercises on a regular basis. In a strange twist of fate, you desire that your muscles adapt! To stimulate muscular growth, a significant stress must be placed on the muscle. As you workout, your muscles will become more used to taking on loads that were previously too much for them. It's not necessary to adjust your workouts once you've achieved the type of muscular growth you seek; rather, you should simply increase the load you exert on the muscle. Repetition, set weight, and rest time may all be used to change this gradual overload. By gradually increasing the strain on the muscle, it will gradually adapt and expand over time. In order to keep your muscles from becoming used to a workout, it is helpful to alter up the sequence in which you perform the exercises in your regimen. It is possible to gradually boost muscle growth by making an adjustment to your workout regimen.

Myth #16: Women gain weight from dieting.

Some female gym-goers are afraid of weight training for fear that it would make them appear chubby, which is a misconception. Unlike men, women are unable to build muscular mass due to a lack of testosterone and growth hormones. Even the tiniest amount of muscle requires a significant amount of effort. Females needn't worry about bulking up with the help of a dumbbell because there are men who practise weight training every day and yet can't gain a pound of muscle. Years of weight training and good diet are necessary for bulking up from weight training. An individual should know how to adapt their workout to get their ideal physique by the time muscular growth becomes visible. Incorporating weight training into your workout routine without bulking up is doable with the right diet and exercise regimen.

Myth #17: Overconsumption of protein.

There are those who dispute how much protein one's system is able to absorb in a given period of time. Many variables influence how your body processes the protein you ingest. When discussing protein intake, it's typical to forget about the other macronutrients that have been ingested before and after. Protein absorption is influenced by the meal's carbohydrate and fat content. It is immaterial how much protein you can absorb in a short period of time if you are not entirely fasting because the body may metabolise some meals for up to three days. Under some circumstances, large quantities of protein are better absorbed and used. The risk of muscle loss is reduced by include more protein in a diet with a calorie deficit. Consuming protein with each meal is a good way to keep amino acids (protein) flowing throughout the day.

Because each person is unique, the amount of protein they need depends on their genetics and body composition. Large men will no longer be restricted to the same protein intake as petite women, thanks to this discovery. Having greater muscle means your body will need more protein. Gluconeogenesis occurs when you ingest more protein than your body requires, resulting in glucose being converted to energy (when in a calorie deficit or at maintenance). During a calorie surplus, an individual should eat a reasonable amount of protein to avoid storing excess protein as fat. As long as your macronutrient needs are met, your body is able to efficiently consume large amounts of protein.

WEIGHING YOUR OWN WEIGHT

Your weight changes throughout the day, therefore the scale will show you various numbers based on the time of day you choose to weigh in. Your weight fluctuates during the day depending on a variety of variables, including the amount of food you consume and the amount of exercise you get. First thing in the morning after urine is the best time to check your weight. Weighing yourself at least once a week might help you monitor your progress toward your weight loss target. Doing so will give you a better sense of how your calorie balance affects your weight, and it's not required to weigh yourself every day.

TOO MUCH WEIGHT LOSS

By ingesting less calories than they burn, a person can lose weight. In only a few days, you may lose several pounds by eating very little and exercising very much. Despite the fact that this is a surefire strategy to lose weight quickly, it may not be the greatest path to pursue. Fat stored in the body is used as a source of energy when the body is in a calorie deficit, when you burn more calories than you ingest. However, your body will use more than just fat as a fuel source if your calorie deficit is excessive. Muscle mass can be lost as a result of the body's increased reliance on protein as a fuel source. When you lose muscle mass, your strength deteriorates, and your physical attractiveness suffers as a result.

Burn as much fat as possible while retaining muscle mass is the objective of weight loss. As a result, losing weight at a steady rate is critical if you want to burn fat effectively. If you drastically reduce your caloric intake, you may end up sacrificing muscle as a source of fuel. If you lose more than 2 pounds a week, you're more likely to lose muscle, say researchers. Losing weight too quickly comes with additional risks, such as poor energy, mood changes, metabolic damage and other undesirable diseases. As a result, losing more than 2 pounds every week is not suggested. The more muscle you have, the slower the speed.

EXERCISES IN THE BODY

It is easier to grasp what happens to your body if you pay more attention to how it feels. Because the primary goal of your body is to keep you alive, it is capable of adapting to whatever situation you subject it to. The goal of the human body is to maintain homeostasis, or equilibrium, at all times. It can be difficult to alter your body's composition due to your body's natural resistance to change. When attempting to shed pounds, we see an example of homeostasis in action. As a result of under-consumption of calories, your body will signal that it is hungry so that you eat more food. Body fat is used for calories if these signals are not addressed. Overeating causes your body to respond by telling you that you're already full, even when you're not. Your body will retain the additional calories as fat if you ignore these cues to quit eating. It's easy to understand how the human body is continually figuring out a method to adapt to new situations.

The amount of water you drink might be a good indicator of how well your body is adapting. People who drink a lot of water in a short amount of time may find themselves making numerous trips to the restroom. Your body eventually adapts to this amount of water, rather than excreting it. When you gradually introduce new conditions to your body, your body will have time to adjust. Because the human body is an intelligent and complicated machine, knowing how it reacts to your efforts to get fit might help you achieve your fitness goals more effectively.

WHERE CAN I FIND WAYS TO SPEED UP THE PROCESS?

In order to see the benefits of your hard work, you may become impatient after a while of working out regularly. To get better results faster, most people think they need to workout more. Though this will help to a certain degree, it is only a portion of the formula to accomplishing your objective. Regardless of whether your aim is to lose weight or gain muscle, the best approach to do it is to create a diet plan. The easiest approach to see results is to make sure that your strategy is correctly set up to achieve your objective and to really stick to it each day. Achieving certain goals may take weeks or even months, but the most important component of success is not squandering any days of effort. It might take twice as long to see effects if you only give your nutrition half of your attention. People who were committed to working toward their goal every day saw some incredible results in their 90-day makeovers. It's up to you whether it takes you 90 days or 180 days if you're only sort of interested.

If you want to see improvement in your training, you need to make sure your programme is set up to do so. Look at everything you're doing and see where you can make improvements in order to reach your goal more quickly. The majority of individuals who are trying to get healthy are more concerned with the workout element than the nutritional part. Faster results can be achieved by dedicating more time to training and adhering to a nutrition plan.

No matter how long it takes to reach your goals, never give up on your dreams because you think it would be too difficult. There is no need to worry about it. " Earl Nightingale, " '

WHICH DIET IS THE BEST?

With so many diets on the market, it can be difficult to know which one is the best for your specific situation. Paleo, Atkins, Vegan, Fruitarian, Ketogenic, gluten-free, and other popular diets are just a few of the most well-known. What's the finest one? The most effective diet is the one one you are most likely to follow through with. They all have the same objective, which is to burn fat. Low-carbohydrate, high fat, whole food, fruit and other controlled principles are common in many diets. A calorie deficit is a fundamental rule of every diet, and it's critical that you remember this regardless of the diet plan that you follow in order to lose weight. The majority of dieters experiment with a variety of diets and restrict a wide range of foods, but they never maintain a calorie deficit over time, which contradicts the objective of dieting.

Tracking your macros eliminates the guesswork of whether or not you're in a calorie deficit by providing you with the precise amount of calories you're consuming. Following a certain diet is much easier if you are aware of your macronutrient intake. Bread, for example, may be a no-no on some diets. A calorie deficit can be caused by cutting back on bread consumption if one previously consumed a lot of bread and then abruptly stopped. The reason you couldn't lose weight was not because you were eating too much bread, but because your overall calorie intake was too high. If you want to lose weight, you may either cut calories by eliminating particular items from your diet or keep track of your intake and eat anything you want in moderation. Make sure your diet consists of items that you love so that you don't become bored. You are more likely to stick with good behaviours if you follow a sustainable diet.

TIME TO FIGHT BETWEEN REFUSE AND CHEAT

People who have been on a restrictive diet for an extended period of time often have cravings for items they wish they could have more of. You may end yourself eating more than you should on a cheat day, delaying your weight loss efforts. In the refeeding community, a "managed cheat day" is a term that describes the practise. Reduces the impulse to overeat and alleviates the stress of long-term dieting by having a refeed A refeed allows a person to consume their maintenance caloric intake (or more) without gaining weight. After a refeed, weight gain is common, but should return to normal within a few days if you continue to diet. The goal of a refeed is to eat more carbs while maintaining your fat and protein intake the same for the whole day. A refeed can help you get back on track when you're experiencing a decline in training performance and low energy levels, or as a reward for sticking to your goals.

Refeeding every week or two throughout a long-term diet might assist prevent plateaus while trying to burn fat for the long run.

TO REACH YOUR OBJECTIVES WITHOUT RECORDING YOUR CALORIE CONSUMPTION

Tracking calories is as straightforward as anybody can make it sound, yet there will always be those who detest the prospect of doing so. It is possible to build a terrific body without tracking your caloric intake, but the outcomes may be less ideal in terms of time, accuracy, weight control, stress, and body composition, among other things. The purpose of this section is to provide you with information on how to avoid counting calories, however keeping track of your calories or macronutrients for 1-2 days will give you an idea of how much you consume on a typical day. The amount of food and liquid you consume from now on can be adjusted based on this value. Half of your plate should be made up of lean protein and starchy carbohydrates, and the rest should be made up of whatever veggies that you choose. Consuming at least your bodyweight in grammes of protein each day is essential for muscle recovery throughout both bulking and reducing phases.

If you want to lose weight without counting calories, the most essential thing is to check your weight each week to see if you're making any progress. The amount of food in your meals may need to be adjusted if you're not seeing the weight loss you'd want. Carbohydrates should be reduced or fat consumption should be limited if you are attempting to lose weight. Continue to monitor your weight throughout the course of the week to see whether you've made any progress with your new portion sizes. A diet high in veggies and low in starchy carbohydrates will help you lose weight by reducing the number of calories you consume each day. Drinking water, coffee, tea, and other calorie-free liquids is a good way to stay healthy.

Increasing one's caloric intake over one's maintenance level is the most important consideration for anyone trying to bulk up. Some people may find it difficult to eat more food than their bodies require on a daily basis. Your body will eventually tell you that you aren't hungry, but the goal is to maintain eating enough to let your body acquire weight. Add additional starchy carbohydrates to your meals if you discover that you aren't gaining weight on a weekly basis. If you overeat because you don't know how many calories you're taking in, you run the risk of gaining more fat than muscle. In order for the weight gain to come from muscle growth, some type of workout must be done. Despite the fact that it is less than ideal to achieve your target without being aware of your calorie intake, following these suggestions will help you get there.

POSSIBILITIES TO IMPROVE YOUR FITNESS

Every day, the internet is inundated with articles and resources aimed at helping you get fitter. Many people have already reached their fitness goals and often share their views and experiences in an effort to assist others in doing the same. Getting advice that can save you time and effort is always a good idea. You can find just about everything on Google, and it's even better for finding fitness advice. One of the greatest ways to learn about exercises, good technique, workout examples, recipes, and a plethora of other fitness-related topics is through the use of YouTube. To find answers to your queries, simply jot them down the next time you're in front of a computer. It's a good idea to check out a variety of sources before taking any advise, just to be safe. Instagram is also a terrific place to get motivational photographs of people with impressive physiques, which may help you stay on track with your objectives. When you don't know the answer to something, use the internet to find out. If you'd like, you can check out some of my favourite fitness-related Youtube channels and websites by clicking on the buttons below.

High-quality material on training, diet, and personal interviews with the best fitness athletes in the world of aesthetics can be found at SimplyShredded.com.

Scott Herman Fitness - Provides step-by-step instructions and video demonstrations on how to do specific exercises correctly.

With the help of his own gym and fitness gear brand "Alphalete," Christian Guzman Fitness is a self-described "ambitious" YouTuber who chronicles his workouts, meals, and business endeavours.

As a fitness fanatic and YouTuber, Nikki Blackketter is a fascinating person to watch.

Brandon Carter - Provides daily videos of home exercises that are both quick and simple, as well as motivational in nature.

Easy-to-follow training videos and nutritious meals may be found on Michael Kory Fitness's YouTube channel.

In order to construct an athletic body, Athlean-X analyses the science behind it. Offers alternate training approaches and critiques individual workouts.

Bodybuilder Rob Riches provides professional guidance and recommendations on how to arrange your diet and workout.

'The Online Coach,' a committed gym owner who posts workouts and fitness tips on a daily basis, is a popular source for daily videos.

It's Twin Muscle Workout - Twin brothers who express their thoughts on a variety of fitness-related topics.

This is the most popular website for knowledge on all things related to muscle growth and fat loss.

Bodybuilder Ulisses World has amazing training guidance and recommendations.

Insight into the world of aesthetic bodybuilding, athletes, and models via Fit Media's Youtube channel.

RELIABLE ADVICE

CUTTING

• Having a cup of coffee a day might help you feel less hungry.

Do not wait too long to begin a weight loss programme. Give your body some time to adjust before comparing the two.

Spicy spices have been demonstrated to help you eat less. •

Foods that may tempt you to deviate from your diet should not be readily available.

Monitor your weight as frequently as possible.

It's been shown that chewing sugarless gum helps reduce sugar cravings

If you want to drink more water, try squeezing fresh lemon juice into your water.

• Keep yourself occupied. You won't be thinking about eating as much if you do this.

More veggies are a great way to obtain more nutrition for less calories.

• Eat at home as much as possible; avoid eating out as much as possible.

Once a week, incorporate one of your favourite foods into your macros.

Consume protein throughout the day to keep your carb consumption under control.

Before each meal, sip a cup of water.

BULKING

Eat items that are high in calories

• Stay hydrated! Increased training need more water.·

• Increase your carbohydrate intake.

• Eat a variety of veggies.

When you're on the run, bring a food with you.

Reduce the amount of cardio you do.

• Train muscular areas that are falling behind.

Be careful to weigh yourself every week to track your progress.

In order to ensure muscular growth, you need often increase the workload of your workouts.

•

TRAINING

Before beginning an exercise, make a plan of action.

• Training time is reduced by short break intervals.

• Make working out a priority instead of an afterthought. •

Prevent injury by practising with appropriate technique before attempting a workout.

· Use momentum sparingly.

If you're going to do intensive cardio, do it after you do weights or on a different day.

• You should always strive to improve upon your previous performance.

• Make a playlist of your favourite songs to keep you motivated.

To keep track of your progress, keep track of the number of sets, repetitions, and weight for each exercise.

Chapter Eight

SUMMARY

There is always room for development in many elements of fitness, including diet and exercise. Nutrition's basics and advantages may be applied to any day-to-day routine. On order to achieve your objective, you must choose between a good diet and an unhealthy diet, and it is this latter choice that will determine how far you get in your journey. Controlling your body composition begins with deciding whether or not to lose, gain, or retain weight. If you don't alter your calorie intake, you will gain weight, lose fat, or stay the same weight.

The human body is incredibly intelligent and can adapt to any method that allows it to perform at its best. You'll be able to achieve your fitness goals faster if you have a better grasp of the science behind your body. It is possible to increase the effectiveness and efficiency of your exercises if you use the training methods and advice offered here. Muscles grow mostly as a result of consistent workout, good diet, and adequate rest. Consistently repeating this cycle is critical to accomplishing your fitness objective, and water is an important part of this process, as well.

Anyone who wants to get in shape can benefit from learning the basic facts about how to burn fat while avoiding the pitfalls of regular diets. The things you love eating should be a part of whatever diet you choose to follow. To get the best results, make sure your dietary choices are in sync with your objectives and stick to a routine. Your body is a checklist that includes specified quantities of macro- and micronutrients as well as water and physical activity each day. Your progress will be accelerated if you are able to regularly complete all of the tasks on your list each day. You'll have more control, flexibility, and self-assurance as you work toward your fitness objective if you understand the connection between what you eat and the daily amount your body receives. This guide will teach you the fundamentals of achieving your ideal physical appearance via a combination of good nutrition and regular exercise.

It's important to keep things honest (PARTING MESSAGE)

Many individuals aspire to have the body of their dreams, but only a select handful are prepared to put in the time and effort it takes to achieve that goal. Reading this book a thousand times and studying fitness topics isn't enough. You must put your knowledge into practise to see results. Many individuals put in a lot of effort year after year to be in shape, but they never seem to see the results they were hoping for. Work hard, but don't forget to work wisely as well. This book is an educational resource written with the goal of assisting you in making a positive impact in your life.

Ask yourself what is preventing you from reaching your ideal physical appearance. Is not having it truly worth the reasons you come up with? It's possible that you just don't want it enough, and that's fine. Even though you have five times as many reasons than this person, you still choose to pursue your health objective. If you've ever seen those 90-day infomercials on TV where individuals lose a tonne of weight and get into shape, you'll know what I mean. Even if those ads are real, it would take far longer than 90 days to attain the results they claim. These adverts are usually real. Even if you give the average individual the identical 90-day weight reduction plan, they may only stick with it for part of it. Rather than 90 days, the person involved would need 180 days to accomplish their goal. All the individuals in infomercials had in common was a relentless pursuit of their goals, one that left them with little time to squander. They honed their physiques by putting in the time and effort required to get them. True to form, here is an example of how the effort you put in is reflected in your output.

Some people work out often in an attempt to improve their physical appearance, but they see little to no improvement in this direction. This is most likely due to the fact that their diet does not support their desired outcome. Consider attempting to cultivate a plant. To grow a seed, you need to bury it in soil, expose it to sunlight, and provide it with a precise amount of water. You are the seed, exercise is the sun, and calories are the water you require to reach your destination. It's possible for some people to get enough exercise (sun) yet drench their bodies with too many or not enough calories (water) that prevents their bodies from developing into the shape they desire. When it comes to your health, you have complete influence over what occurs. The quickest way to see results is to train hard and eat precisely on a regular basis. For the most part, the normal individual is unable to accomplish their goal because they have too many reasons for not doing so. Identify yourself as an individual who is above and above the typical human.

Achieving a goal provides you the self-assurance to carry out any promise you make to yourself. You may challenge yourself to be a better person while directly reaping the benefits of your hard work and consistency via fitness. You won't see everyone strolling around with a flawless body since achieving your fitness goals is difficult. Avoid becoming too comfortable in your current situation, since this will prevent you from growing as a person. The human body prefers to do nothing and will only undergo change if compelled to do so. Having a positive attitude can help you overcome whatever obstacles you may encounter. The only person standing in the way of attaining any personal ambitions is you.

INTERNET FITNESS TRAINING.

Taking the initial step toward attaining your fitness goal might be difficult. A lack of motivation may be holding you back from pursuing your goal, or you may know where to begin but lack the will to keep going. With or without a specific goal in mind, hiring a personal trainer may be a terrific approach to get the body and lifestyle that you desire. Your personal nutrition and/or training will eliminate any guesswork from the process and ensure that you are effectively achieving the body that you desire. The only thing you have to do is stick to a schedule and stay motivated. Having a coach can help you achieve your fitness goals in the following ways:

It doesn't matter whether your aim is to reduce weight, gain muscle mass, or do both; a plan will be created to meet your needs and goals specifically. An individual's body type and amount of physical activity are taken into account when creating a macronutrient intake and/or meal plan.

With every objective, having the willpower to keep going is essential to success. With a coach who keeps you motivated and engaged throughout the programme, you are less likely to get bored or lose concentration.

Everyone's lifestyle and schedule might clash with their aim, so it's important to keep this in mind. Instead of tailoring your lifestyle to your diet, your diet will be based on your lifestyle and what is most convenient for you to follow. If you enjoy eating traditional foods, a coach can help you consume them in the right quantities to keep you on track toward your goal.

Customized macros allow you to eat as many calories as possible while keeping on track to meet your fitness goal.

Having a coach to keep you accountable can help you stay focused on your objective. Coaches are there to help you if you have any "slip-ups" on your diet.

To help clear up any misunderstandings, individuals provide their honest perspectives on nutrition and fitness. In order to continue success, coaches might share their own experiences and provide alternate dietary options.

With a coach, you'll be able to stay on track and reach your goals on time, whether they're related to a special event like a wedding or vacation. Instead of winging it and crossing your fingers, working with a coach will get you where you want to go faster.

Along the process, you'll learn about nutrition and how to incorporate it into your exercise routines. By doing this, you can prevent yourself from reverting to your old behaviours once you've achieved your goal. In order to successfully transition into a healthy lifestyle, you'll need the aid of a coach.

Raspberry muffins

The phytonutrient rheosmin, which is also known as raspberry ketone, is found in raspberries (pronounced key-tone). It has been found that this enzyme can speed up the process of losing weight. If you're looking to reduce weight while enjoying a guilt-free muffin, look no further!

Contains enough food for a dozen people.

Ingredients

A half-cup of raspberries

1/2 cup of rolled oats

1 cup of 1 percent low-fat milk

3.5 ounces of all-purpose flour

A quarter-cup of grits

1/4 cup of wheat bran

One spoonful of baking powder.

1/4 teaspoon of salt

1 1/2 cups of dark honey

3 1/2 teaspoons of olive oil

Lime zest.....2 tablespoons grated

The gentle beating of one egg

Directions

The oven should be preheated at 400 degrees Fahrenheit (200 degrees Celsius). Line a 12-cup muffin tin with wax paper or aluminium foil liners before baking.

The milk and oats are mixed together in a medium pot. Until the oats are soft and the mixture is creamy, cook and stir over medium heat. After cooking, remove from heat and leave aside while you go on with the rest of the steps in the recipe.

Baked goods can be made with a variety of different grains and flours.

Whisk the eggs in a small dish and set them aside.

Combine the oats with the honey, olive oil, and lime zest before stirring in the remaining ingredients. Eggs can be added at this point if desired. The batter should be wet yet lumpy when finished. The raspberries should be incorporated into the mixture with care.

Scoop the batter into the muffin tins with one tablespoon and push it in with the other, filling each cup about three-quarters full.

Bake for 16 to 18 minutes, or until the tops are golden brown. As long as the centre is completely clean, you can insert a toothpick there. Return the muffins to the oven for a few more minutes if the dough adheres to the toothpick.

Allow the muffins to cool fully before serving on a wire rack.

Per serving, this is the nutrient breakdown.

One muffin serves as a serving.

27 grammes of carbs total.

Fibre in the diet, 2 grammes

126 mg of sodium

0.5 g of saturated fat per serving

5 g of total fat

Amount of trans fat less than 0.5

16 mg of cholesterol

3 g of protein

3 g of monounsaturated fat

165 calories are the recommended daily calorie intake.

Amount of sugar: 11 g

Buckwheat Pancakes with Strawberries

Buckwheat is actually a fruit seed and not a cereal grain. It is linked to the rhubarb and sorrel family which makes it an excellent replacement for folks who have allergies to wheat or other cereals.

Serves 6

Ingredients

Egg whites.....2

Olive oil.....1 tbsp

Fat-free milk.....1/2 cup

All purpose flour.....1/2 cup

Buckwheat flour.....1/2 cup

Baking powder.....1 tbsp

Sparkling water.....1/2 cup

Fresh strawberries.....3 cups cut

Directions

In a large dish mix together the egg whites, olive oil and milk.

In another basin add the all-purpose flour, buckwheat flour and baking powder and stir completely.

Slowly add the dry ingredients to the egg white mixture while you alternately add the sparkling water. Make sure to stir between each addition until all the ingredients blend into a batter.

Place a nonstick frying pan or griddle over medium heat. Spoon 1/2 cup of the pancake batter into the pan. Cook until the top surface of the pancake bubbles and the edges turn gently golden, about 2 minutes. Flip and heat until the bottom is attractively brown and cooked through, 1 to 2 minutes more. Repeat with the remaining pancake batter.

Transfer the pancakes to individual plates. Top each with 1/2 cup cut strawberries. Serve.

Amount of nutrients in per serving

A single pancake is the recommended serving size.

Weight in grammes: 24 g of carbs

3 g of fibre in your diet

150 mg of sodium

Fat containing traces of saturated fatty acids

3 grammes of fat total.

Traces of cholesterol

5 g of protein

2 g of monounsaturated fatty acids

There are 143 calories in a single serving.

Chapter Nine

LUNCH

Pizza with Sun-Dried Tomatoes and Basil

Lycopene, vitamin C, and antioxidants are all found in sun-dried tomatoes. Tomato paste and puree are common applications for them. It is common to see sun-dried goods made using red plum tomatoes.

Serves four

Ingredients

a single 12 inch pre-made pizza crust from a mix or baked at home

Cloves of garlic...4

A half cup of fat-free ricotta cheese

Sun-dried tomatoes put in a vacuum-sealed container...

2 teaspoons of dried basil

1-teaspoon Thyme

Pepper flakes with a reddish hue

a kind of cheese known as parmesan.

Directions

A 475 °F (250 °C) oven temperature is ideal.

Apply cooking spray to a 12-inch round pizza pie baking pan.

Before utilising sun-dried tomatoes, they must be rehydrated. Then cover them with hot water until they're completely submerged. Keep at room temperature for 5 minutes, or until pliable. Chopping and dredging

The pizza crust should be placed in a circular pizza pie pan before baking. Top the pizza dough with the garlic, cheese, and tomatoes. Add a generous amount of fresh basil and thyme to the pizza and toss to coat.

The toppings should be hot and the crust browned on the bottom of the oven, which should take around 20 minutes.

Immediately slice the pizza into eight equal pieces and serve to your guests.

For individual usage, place the red-flaked pepper jar and the parmesan container on the counter.

Amount of nutrients in per serving

Size of serving: 2 pieces

2 grammes of fat are included in the total.

179 calories are the recommended daily calorie intake.

8 g of protein

8 milligrammes of cholesterol per deciliter of blood

32 grammes of carbs total

fibre in the diet, 2 g

0.5 grammes of monounsaturated fat

Fat containing traces of saturated fatty acids

276 milligrammes of sodium

White Wine and Mushroom-Smothered Chicken

As a source of protein, chicken is excellent. 30 grammes of protein are found in 100 grammes of chicken. Comparatively, if you eat 100 grammes of tuna, salmon or halibut, you'll get 26 grammes of protein.

It's a terrific recipe to serve with spaghetti. Make your supper complete by serving it with a side of fresh-steamed veggies.

Serves four

Ingredients

Chicken breasts, boneless and skinless, 4 to 4 ounces each

2 teaspoons of extra virgin olive oil

4 slices of finely cut shallots

1/4 pound of finely sliced mushrooms.

One tablespoon of all-purpose flour

A quarter cup of white wine.

Low-sodium chicken stock...1/2 cup

1 Tablespoon of fresh rosemary (or 1 teaspoon dried rosemary)

2 Tbsp. chopped fresh parsley.

Directions

Use a mallet or a rolling pin to flatten the chicken breasts after sealing them in a Ziploc bag.

Cut the chicken in half lengthwise once it has been removed from the oven. Ziploc bag and chill until solid.

Prepare two frying pans with one teaspoon of olive oil each for cooking the chicken after it has firmed up.

Whisk the flour and wine together in a small bowl until all the flour lumps have been removed. Remove from sight.

Turn on medium heat in both frying pans. Add the chicken breasts to the first frying pan. Sauté the shallots in the second frying pan for about 3 minutes.

Return to the first frying pan and flip the chicken breasts over, if necessary.

Add the mushrooms and shallots to the second frying pan. For another 2 minutes, stir while the two are sautéing together.

Get the flour and wine mixture in the bowl. Whisk a couple of times, then pour over the shallots and mushrooms. Stir in the chicken stock once you've added the rest of the ingredients.

It should be golden on all sides and cooked thoroughly, with no pink showing, in the first pan. Place on a serving platter when the heat has been turned off.

Return to the pan with the mushrooms and shallots and swirl to ensure that the sauce has thickened to your liking. Mixture should be spooned over chicken once the burner has been turned off.

Serve immediately, garnished with fresh parsley.

Amount of nutrients in per serving

2 chicken breast halves per serving

9 grammes of fat

There are 239 calories in one serving.

28 g of protein

Cholesterol was 66 mg per deciliter.

6 grammes of carbs total

0.5% of your daily value comes from this source:

Omega-3 fatty acids 5 g

The following is the nutritional breakdown of saturated fat:

98 milligrammes of sodium

Dinner

Pineapple and Balsamic Chicken Salad

Free radicals in the pineapple help to combat colds, build stronger bones, and promote gum health in this meal, which has protein-rich chicken. Pineapple also has anti-inflammatory and antioxidant compounds that are beneficial to the heart. Vitamin C, which boosts immunity and lowers blood pressure, is also found in pineapple.

Contains enough food for eight people

Ingredients

Breast of chicken.. Approximately 5 ounces each of boneless, skinless

One tablespoon of olive oil.

pieces of unsweetened pineapple, drained of all but 2 tablespoons of liquid, 1-8 ounce can

2 cups of florets of broccoli

4 cups of fresh baby spinach leaves

1/2 cup finely sliced red onions

When making vinaigrette, follow these steps:

One-quarter cup of olive oil

Two teaspoons of balsamic vinegar

Sugar... 2 teaspoons.

One-fourth teaspoon of cinnamon

Directions

On a medium heat, warm the oil in a big, nonstick frying pan.

Cut each breast into cubes, one at a time.

Cook the chicken in the hot olive oil for 10 minutes or until it is golden brown.

Combine the cooked chicken, sliced onions, pineapple pieces, broccoli, and spinach in a large serving dish and mix well.

Vinaigrette:

Olive oil, vinegar, and the pineapple juice that was set aside are all combined in a bowl. Cinnamon and sugar, if using, should be combined here. Pour the dressing over the salad and gently toss to distribute the dressing evenly. Serve right away.

Amount of nutrients in per serving

8 g of carbs per serving

fibre in the diet, 2 g

Sodium content of 75 milligrammes

The following is the nutritional breakdown of saturated fat:

9 grammes of fat

Total Cholesterol 41 mg

17 g of protein

Six grammes of monounsaturated fat

There are 181 calories in this dish.

Salmon with Tarragon and Chives Roasted

Among the many nutrients included in salmon are: vitamins B3, B6, and B12, protein, phosphorus, choline, pantothenic acid, and biotin. Each one of these vitamins and minerals is necessary for a strong cardiovascular system as well as strong joints, healthy eyes, and a lower chance of developing cancer.

Servings Per Container: 2

Ingredients

2 to 5 ounce slices of organic skin-on salmon

2 teaspoons of extra virgin olive oil, preferably organic.

Chopped chives...1 tbsp

Teaspoonfuls of fresh tarragon

Spray for preparing food in the kitchen

Directions

A 475 °F (250 °C) oven temperature is ideal.

Spritz a baking sheet with nonstick cooking spray and cover it with aluminium foil.

2 teaspoons of extra virgin olive oil rubbed all over the fish.

Roast the fish for 12 minutes with the skin side down, or until it is cooked through.

Lift the salmon's skin using a metal spatula. Place the salmon on a platter for serving. Skin should be thrown away. Serve the fish topped with fresh herbs.

Amount of nutrients in per serving

Carbohydrates - traces

Fiber - a nutrient in food

Sodium content of 62 milligrammes

2 g of saturated fat

14 grammes of fat were consumed in total.

78 milligrammes of cholesterol

28 g of protein

7 grammes of monounsaturated fat

There are 241 calories in one serving.

Salads

Salad with Vegetables in an Asian Style

In terms of beta-carotene and vitamin A, Bok Choy is the most nutritious cabbage kind.

Reduce your risk of heart disease by eating more carrots. Carrots are commonly associated with the colour "orange," but there are fifteen other shades to choose from!

We're told to load up on the brightly hued veggies. It's hard to find a vegetable with a more eye-catching hue than red cabbage. The antioxidant and anti-inflammatory effects of the veggies are enhanced by the red colour.

Serves four

Ingredients

Half a cup of shredded carrots

A half-cup of chopped red bell pepper

One-and-a-half cups chopped Bok Choy

A half-cup of chopped yellow onion

1 cup of sliced red cabbage

1 12 cups of spinach

One tablespoon of minced garlic

One tablespoon of chopped cilantro

1 12 tablespoons of cashews

1 12 cups snow peas

2 tablespoons of low-sodium soy sauce

Directions

Rinse the veggies in cool water and then drain.

Be sure to thinly slice all of the vegetables before adding them to your dish.

Slice the cabbage and spinach into thin strips by cutting them against the grain with a knife.

Chop the garlic finely. Slightly bigger chunks of cashews and cilantro should be cut.

Gather all of the ingredients for the salad together in a large bowl. Soy sauce should be slathered on top. Toss the ingredients together thoroughly before storing in an airtight container. Serve.

Amount of nutrients in per serving

Serving size: approximately 2 cups

Carbohydrates in total: 14 grammes

4 g of dietary fibre

173mg of sodium

The following is the nutritional breakdown of saturated fat:

4 grammes of fat total.

0 g of trans fat

Cholesterol is 0 mg per deciliter.

Phosphorus 3 grammes

2 g of monounsaturated fatty acids

Salad with Mangoes and Cucumbers

Mangoes have been shown to be beneficial in the battle against a variety of malignancies. Vitamin A, beta-carotene, alpha-carotene, beta-cryptoxanthin, potassium, vitamin B6, C, E, and copper are all found in these foods.

Salads like this one go well with roasted chicken or chicken salad as well as Asian veggies and pasta salads.

This recipe yields six servings.

Ingredients

3 pitted and diced mangoes

1 freshly squeezed lime

1 tbsp. minced red onion

HALF of a jalapeno pepper...seeds and everything.

Directions

A mixing bowl works well for this. Refrigerate for ten minutes with the cover on. Before serving, toss the salad.

Amount of nutrients in per serving

There are 19 grammes of carbs in this dish

fibre in the diet, 2 g

10 milligrammes of sodium

Fat containing traces of saturated fatty acids

Fatty acid profile

Cholesterol is 0 mg per deciliter.

1 g of protein per serving

A trace amount of monounsaturated fat.

75 caloric energy

Chapter Ten

APPETIZERS

Bruschetta with Tomato and Basil

If you're attempting to shed some pounds, tomatoes are a great option. They're also helpful in the fight against cancer. The longer you cook a tomato, the more nutrients it has. This is an amazing fact about the tomato. The nutritious content of most fruits and vegetables diminishes over time, but not in the case of the tomato.

This recipe yields six servings.

Ingredients

Half of a whole grain baguette is sliced diagonally into six half-inch thick pieces.

2 Tbsp. chopped fresh basil

1 tablespoon chopped fresh parsley

2 minced garlic cloves

Three diced tomatoes.

Fennel, chopped into a half-cup serving

...1 teaspoon of olive oil

2-teaspoons of balsamic vinegar

To taste: 1 teaspoon freshly ground black pepper

Three teaspoons of Parmesan cheese

Directions

Toss the tomatoes onto a medium-sized dish and chop them into small pieces. Sliced fennel and chopped basil and parsley are other good additions to this dish. Stir. Refrigerate for at least 20 minutes to let the flavours to come together.

Make a 400-degree oven (200-degree C) a priority.

Slice the whole grain baguette diagonally into half-inch thick pieces. Put it in the oven on a baking pan. Using a toaster, toast the baguettes to a golden brown. While still warm from the oven, top with grated parmesan cheese. Take a serving tray and put the salsa on it.

Using a spoon, put the tomato basil combination onto the dish and serve. Serve right away.

Amount of nutrients in per serving

Slices per serving: one

Compound sugars: 20 grammes

4 g of dietary fibre

123 milligrammes of sodium

Saturated fat content 0.5 g

2 grammes of fat are included in the total.

0 g of trans fat

Cholesterol is 0 mg per deciliter.

Phosphorus 3 grammes

It contains 1 g of monounsaturated fat

110 caloric intake

Sugars have a calorie count of 0 g.

Fruit Kebabs with Lemony Lime Dip

Pineapples offer several advantages. They inhibit free radicals from forming, they have anti-inflammatory and anti-cancer properties and they aid to avoid atherosclerosis.

Strawberries are packed of nutrients and help lessen the chance of acquiring Type-2 diabetes.

Kiwi provides phytonutrients that preserve DNA. Kiwi is also a good source of fibre as well as other minerals.

Potassium is a well-known advantage of the banana.

Red grapes contain a comprehensive array of heart-healthy elements that include decreasing blood pressure and cholesterol levels.

Serves 2

Ingredients

Low-fat sugar-free lemon yoghurt.....4 ounces

Lime.....1 for 1 teaspoon lime juice

Lime zest.....1 teaspoon

Pineapple chunks.....4 to 6

Kiwi.....1 peeled and diced

Banana.....1/2 sliced into 1/2-inch slices

Red grapes.....4 to 6

Wooden skewers.....4

Directions

In a small bowl mix together the lemon yoghurt, lime juice and lime zest. Cover and refrigerate to enable the flavours to marinade as you make the rest of the dish.

Using a skewer, insert one piece of each fruit. You may repeat this process with the remaining skewers until all of the fruit has been used up. You may keep your kiwi fruit from browning by putting it near to the pineapple or grapes, but keep it away from the banana.

Make sure to accompany your dish with the zesty lime dip.

Dip fruit in pineapple or orange juice to keep it from becoming brown.

Amount of nutrients in per serving

a serving of 2 fruit kebabs is plenty.

One gramme of fat

calorie intake: 160

4 g of protein

4 milligrammes of cholesterol

36 grammes of carbs in total.

4 g of dietary fibre

trace amounts of monounsaturated fat

Under 1 g of saturated fat

Sodium content of 45 mg.

Dips, Sauces, and Dressings

Dip made with artichokes

When it comes to soothing the stomach, artichokes are excellent. Artichokes may also help lower cholesterol levels, according to studies. You should speak with your doctor before consuming artichokes if you suffer from gallstones. Artichokes are in the same family as ragweed, chrysanthemums, marigolds, and daises, so talk to your doctor if you have any of those allergies.

8 people

Ingredients

2-cup servings of artichoke hearts

4 cups of finely chopped spinach

1 teaspoon minced thyme

2 minced cloves of garlic

One tablespoon of minced fresh parsley.

1 cup cooked white beans

2 tbsp. grated Parmesan

1/2 cup fat-free sour cream

1 Tablespoon of freshly ground black pepper

Directions

Make sure your oven is preheated at 350 °F

A big dish is ideal for this task. Bake for 20 minutes after transferring to a glass or ceramic pan.

For dipping, serve the soup with whole-grain breads and crackers, or veggies like celery.

Amount of nutrients in per serving

Portion size: around half a cup

Carbohydrates in total: 14 grammes

6 grammes of dietary fibre per day

71 milligrammes of sodium

1 g of saturated fat

2 g of total fat

Glycemic index 0

6 mg of cholesterol

5 g of protein

One gramme of monounsaturated fatty acid

There are 94 calories in one serving.

Sugars contain 0 g.

Smear of peach honey on toast

Vitamins, minerals, protein, and beta-carotene abound in peaches, all of which may reduce your risk of cancer. Peaches' high fibre content aids digestion. As a result of the peach's alkaline content, it helps to alleviate digestive issues, and it also has cholesterol-lowering qualities.

Pancakes, waffles, roasted pork, chicken, and even toast go well with this flavorful spread.

This recipe yields six servings.

Ingredients

1 cup of chopped fresh cranberries

1 – 15 ounce can drained of unsweetened peach halves

12 cup of honey

1/2 tsp. of cinnamon

Directions

Chop the drained, unsweetened peach halves in a food processor or blender. Transfer the peaches to a big bowl once they've reached an applesauce-like consistency. Toss the peaches with the honey and cinnamon and serve. Use a big spoon to thoroughly combine the ingredients.

Refrigerate until ready to serve, or reheat and spoon over your favourite food before enjoying.

Amount of nutrients in per serving

Size of serving: one-third of a cup

Fatty acids: 0 g

calorie count: sixty-five

0.5 g of protein

Cholesterol levels in this patient were found to be 0 mg.

Carbohydrates in total: 16 grammes

1 g of dietary fibre

fats monounsaturated 0 g

0 g of saturated fat

4 milligrammes of sodium

How to Consume Less Sodium

Your salt consumption will likely be reduced merely by eating the DASH diet's recommended foods, which are naturally low in sodium.

The following are some more suggestions for lowering your salt intake:

When cooking rice, hot porridge, or pasta, avoid using salt in the water.

Use non-sodium spices, flavourings, or condiments in place of salt in your cooking whenever possible.

Shop for "sodium-free" products, as well as "low sodium" and "no-salt-added" items.

Reduce salt content by rinsing canned goods.

The salt shaker you usually keep on your dinner table should be thrown away

Look at the nutrition facts on food packages.

You may be startled to see how much salt is in processed food if you pay attention to product labels. Sodium levels might be high even in foods that you believe to be healthy. Canned veggies and low-fat soups, for example, are two examples of meals with surprising salt content.

How much sodium is included in salt?

When it comes to sodium content, table salt has an estimated 2300 mg per teaspoon and little over 1500 mg every 2/3 teaspoon.

Foods with a lower salt content

Make a more gradual transition to low-sodium meals if what you regularly eat is too bland when you eat it in "low-sodium" form. Be patient; it will all work out in the end. Getting acclimated to reduced salt diets might take a few months.

Chapter Eleven

THE EIGHT DAY

An Eight-Day Meal Routine

Beginning on the first day

Afternoon Tea: (442 Cal Total)

3/4 cup wheat flakes, shredded (125 Cal)

Organic low-fat milk (100 Cal)

Cereal with one sliced banana (105 Cal)

1 cup of orange juice, freshly squeezed (112 Cal)

Drink one 8-ounce glass of water to start (0 Cal)

Snack of the Day: (200 Cal)

Chopped walnuts, about a quarter cup (200 Cal)

What's for dinner? (311 Cal)

Small boneless and skinless grilled chicken breast (141 Cal)

There are 170 calories in two slices of whole wheat or whole grain bread (85 each).

1-teaspoon mustard made with Dijon (0 Cal)

Composition of a Salad (29 Cal)

Cucumber slices in half a cup (8 Cal)

Half a cup of sliced tomatoes (16 Cal)

1-tablespoon Italian Dressing (low-fat, low-sodium) (5 Cal)

1 glass of water (about 8 ounces) (0)

Afternoon Snack (152 Cal)

3 tbsp. plain, nonfat yoghurt (22 Cal)

Riesling, 14 cup (130 Cal)

There will be a meal: (645)

Top sirloin steak, 3 ounces in weight, roughly the size of a standard deck of cards (158 Cal)

Green beans, cooked to desired tenderness, 1 cup (44 Cal)

Baked potato of a tiny size (145 Cal)

Extra virgin olive oil, about a half-cup (60 Cal)

Dessert is one little apple (116 Cal)

1 cup of milk with a 1% fat content (122 Cal)

Drink one 8-ounce glass of water to start (0 Cal)

Calories in total: 1779

Day two

Afternoon Tea: (377 Cal)

cinnamon-spiced half a cup of regular oats (150 Cal)

A medium banana is all that is needed (105 Cal)

2 percent low-fat milk (122 Cal)

1 cup of plain water (0 Cal)

Snack of the Day: (160 Cal)

Sunflower seeds in a quarter cup (160 Cal)

What's for dinner? (617 Cal)

Chicken salad with 3 ounces of chicken (100 Cal)

Up to 2 cups of Romaine lettuce may be made out of a single Romaine leaf (15 Cal)

Diced tomato is added to the salad for flavour (16 Cal)

As much as 1 cup of chopped celery can be added to the salad (18 Cal)

1 finely sliced green onion, to be used in salad (10 Cal)

Salad with 1 tablespoon of low-fat mayonnaise (35 Cal)

Whole wheat or multi grain bread two pieces (180 Cal, one slice is 90 Cal)

The cheese is a single piece (66 Cal)

1 cup of chopped cantaloupe (60 Cal)

Apple juice in the amount of 1 cup (117 Cal)

Drink 8 oz. of water (0 Cal)

Afternoon Snack (152.5 Cal)

Dried apricots in 1/4 cup measure (100 Cal)

3 tblsp. plain yoghurt with Greek yoghurt (52.5 Cal)

There will be a meal: (356 Cal)

1 cup of wheat pasta (174 Cal)

a cup and a half of mushrooms (22 Cal)

No meat in this half cup of spaghetti sauce (45 Cal)

Parmigiano-Reggiano is 3 tablespoons of cheese (63 Cal)

1 pound of chard (7 Cal)

1 medium carrot, grated (25 Cal)

The fat-free Italian salad dressing has 2 tablespoons (20 Cal)

A total of 1662.5 calories

The third day has come.

Afternoon Tea: (449 Cal)

Approximately 2 cups of finely puffed wheat (100 Cal)

A medium banana is all that is needed (105 Cal)

1 cup of low-fat milk with a 2% fat content (122 Cal)

1 cup orange juice straight from the squeezer (122 Cal)

Drink 8 oz. of water (0 Cal)

Snack of the Day: (238 Cal)

Greek vanilla yoghurt in a cup (170 Cal)

Blueberries, about a cup (21 Cal)

1 tablespoon sunflower seeds, no salt added (47 Cal) (47 Cal)

What's for dinner? (460 Cal)

Sandwich of grilled flounder, 3 ounces (100 Cal)

2 percent milk, 1 piece of cheese (45 Cal)

1 whole-wheat bread for a hamburger (200 Cal)

The size of a huge Romaine lettuce leaf (15 Cal)

1 tbsp. light mayonnaise, whipped (35 Cal)

An orange the size of your fist (65 Cal)

Drink 8 oz. of water (0 Cal)

Afternoon Snack (308 Cal)

Graham crackers, 2 big (118 Cal, each large rectangle or 2 squares is 59 Cal Ea.)

It doesn't matter if you want your peanut butter smooth or crunchy (190 Cal)

There will be a meal: (248 Cal)

Fresh tuna, 3 ounces (118 Cal)

a tablespoon of lemon juice (22 Cal)

1 cup of spinach, cooked (41 Cal)

1 muffin of bran (67 Cal)

Drink 8 oz. of water (0 Cal)

The total number of calories consumed was 1703.

Breakfast on Day 4: (404 Cal)

2 tablespoons of blueberries in 1 cup of Greek yoghurt (80 Cal)

This is a medium-sized peach (40 Cal)

Whole grain toast, one slice (69 Cal)

1-tablespoon low-fat margarine without salt (45 Cal)

Welch's pure purple grape juice in an 8 oz. glass (170 Cal)

Drink 8 oz. of water (0 Cal)

Snack of the Day: (281 Cal)

The equivalent of 24 almonds is 1 ounce (164 Cal)

a half cup of apple juice (117 Cal)

What's for dinner? (316 Cal)

Sandwich made with 2 ounces of extra lean 5 percent fat ham and 1 slice of 2 percent fat cheese (60 calories) equals a ham and cheese sandwich (45 calories) (105 Cal)

For the sandwich, use two pieces of whole-grain bread (120 Cal)

The size of a huge Romaine lettuce leaf (15 Cal)

a half-a-tomato (16 Cal)

Mayonnaise with a reduced fat content of 1 teaspoon (35 Cal)

a medium-sized carrot that has been sliced into sticks (25 Cal)

Drink 8 oz. of water (0 Cal)

Afternoon Snack (139 Cal)

Apricot, one (17 Cal)

1 cup of fat-free or low-fat milk (122 Cal)

There will be a meal: (585 Cal)

Skinless and boneless breast of chicken (150 Cal)

1 cup medium grain brown rice (150 Cal)

1 cup boiling green peas (124 Cal)

4 oz. slices of cantaloupe (39 Cal)

1 cup of fat-free or low-fat milk (122 Cal)

Weight in pounds – 1725.

The fifth day of the challenge.

Afternoon Tea: (669 Cal)

3/4 cup wheat flakes, shredded (125 Cal)

A medium banana is all that is needed (105 Cal)

A single bagel (110 Cal)

To make the bagel, use 1 teaspoon of peanut butter (95 Cal)

1 cup of fat-free or low-fat milk (122 Cal)

1 quart of orange juice (112 Cal)

Drink 8 oz. of water (0 Cal)

Snack of the Day: (94 Cal)

2 tbsp. of unsalted sunflower seed (94 Cal)

What's for dinner? (565 Cal)

2 ounces of albacore tuna (70 Cal)

Mayonnaise with a reduced fat content of 1 teaspoon (35 Cal)

lettuce leaf from the romaine variety (15 Cal)

1 piece of whole grain or wheat bread (85 Cal)

One cucumber is all that is needed to make a cucumber salad (8 Cal)

...1/2 cup of chopped tomato (16 Cal)

Vinaigrette:... 2 tablespoons of red wine vinegar (70 Cal)

2 percent low-fat cottage cheese....4oz - (102 Cal)

...1 ounce of unsalted almonds (164 Cal)

Drink 8 oz. of water (0 Cal)

Afternoon Snack (91 Cal)

Strawberry low-fat yoghurt (91 Cal)

There will be a meal: (551 Cal)

3-4 ounces of ground turkey meatloaf (120 Cal)

Baked potato of a tiny size (129 Cal)

2 percent low-fat shredded cheddar 1 tablespoon (80 Cal)

Collards, about a cupful (49 Cal)

The equivalent of a tiny piece of whole wheat bread (114 Cal)

This is a medium-sized peach (59 Cal)

Drink 8 oz. of water (0 Cal)

Amount of calories consumed per day in 1970

On the sixth day,

Afternoon Tea: (417 Cal)

1 granola bar low in fat - (110 Cal)

A medium banana is all that is needed (105 Cal)

Strawberries and bananas in a low-fat yoghurt (80 Cal)

1 cup of milk with 2% fat content (122 Cal)

8 oz. of water (0 Cal)

Snack of the Day: (160 Cal)

Sunflower seeds in a quarter cup (160 Cal)

What's for dinner? (404 Cal)

chicken breast, 3 ounces, cooked (100 Cal)

a loaf of whole wheat bread with two pieces (138 Cal - 69 Cal ea.)

1 Romaine lettuce leaf, chopped up (15 Cal)

a half-a-tomato (16 Cal)

Low-fat mayonnaise, 2 tablespoons (70 Cal - 35 Cal ea.)

A single piece of orange (65 Cal)

Drink 8 oz. of water (0 Cal)

Afternoon Snack (17 Cal)

1 whole apricot (17 Cal)

There will be a meal: (395 Cal)

1 wild-caught fillet of trout (215 Cal)

1 cup of spinach, cooked (41 Cal)

A single piece of carrot (25 Cal)

1 small dinner roll made with whole wheat (114 Cal)

8 oz. of water (0 Cal)

1393 calories are the total.

The seventh day.

Afternoon Tea: (341 Cal)

Oatmeal with cinnamon is 150 calories for half a cup. Sixty-six calories

A medium banana is all that is needed (105 Cal)

2 tablespoons of maple syrup (80 Cal)

Drink 8 oz. of water (0 Cal)

Snack of the Day: (164 Cal)

1 ounce of unsalted almonds (164 Cal)

What's for dinner? (443 Cal)

Sandwich made using 2 ounces of solid albacore tuna (70 Cal)

1 tbsp. light mayonnaise, whipped (35 Cal)

a medium-sized head of lettuce (15 Cal)

a half-a-tomato (16 Cal)

a loaf of whole grain bread (120 Cal - 1 slice is 60 Cal)

A single piece of orange (65 Cal)

1 cup of milk with 2% fat content (122 Cal)

8 oz. of water (0 Cal)

Afternoon Snack (182 Cal)

Seven slices of whole wheat bread (120 Cal)

1 cup of seedless white or purple grapes (62 Cal)

There will be a meal: (478 Cal)

3 ounces of unseasoned, charred shrimp skewers (101 Cal)

1 cup of fresh spinach equals 1 salad (7 Cal)

1 cup of chopped tomato (16 Cal)

vinaigrette made with red wine, 2 tbsp (70 Cal)

Rolls made with whole wheat or multigrain (114 Cal)

8 ounces of a grape juice concentrate (170 Cal)

8 oz. of water (0 Cal)

1608 calories are the total amount of calories in this recipe.

Limiting the Amount Consumed and the Amount Served

The DASH diet emphasises the significance of sensible portion control, a wide range of meals, and adequate nutritional intake.

Eating too much is more often than not the culprit rather than the food itself.

Measuring your meals is a pain, but it's necessary if you want to make sure you're getting enough of each food group throughout the day.

When you eat, how do you get into the habit of calculating out your portions?

It wasn't until I started breaking down store-bought packets a long time ago that I realised I was re-packaging goods in unacceptably enormous quantities for my own and my family's servings.

To motivate myself, I would tell myself to make sure there was enough food for everyone in the house before starting the repackaging process. My attention was drawn to what we did with the wrapped leftovers.

We ate more than we should have because we didn't use them for what I had meant.

Discovering that what you truly need and what you consume are two completely different things is astounding.

The diagnosis of diabetes in my spouse gradually ushered us into a new era of family eating habits. We learned new behaviours as a result of his heart attack and insulin issues, which led to our own food concerns.

Prior to purchasing food, I had to learn how to read food labels. In order to answer this question, I had to try the dish. My estimation of my own value shifted dramatically in the course of what felt like a single day. My eyes were opened to the need of consuming foods that are rich in nutrients rather than those that are low in nutrients.

I began portioning up my snacks and putting them in Ziploc bags to keep them fresh. You didn't have to perform the arithmetic every time you wanted a snack because of this. As far as I know, it had previously been solved.

Instead of creating extra for one or two meals, I divided our meat packages into two, three, or even four distinct meal plans. Snacks are what they are, and meals are what they are.

My spouse used to cook a double-decker sandwich as a snack. I miss those days. We've come a long way since those days, and we now understand that a snack is simply a snack.

Using what you already have in the cupboard, refrigerator, and freezer is a good place to start your "portion size repackaging efforts."

When you start looking at serving sizes, you'll discover several things about what constitutes a serving that you didn't expect.

Learn as much as you can about the foods you eat, including the methods used to produce them. Purchasing and chopping your own fresh fruit may help you consume more of it. Why? It's because the chemicals in processing increase the calorie content while decreasing the serving size. Sugar is commonly used as a preservative when fruits are canned. This reduces the size of the portion.

To prevent the fruit from rotting, yoghurt manufacturers are required to add extra ingredients to yoghurt when it is sold with actual fruit. Typically, this is a sugar-based syrup. Buying plain yoghurt and sprinkling your own fruit on top is a superior option.

Calories and serving sizes permitted by the DASH diet

In the DASH diet, each food category is recommended to be consumed at least once a day. Calorie intake has been divided into three tiers, each with its own serving size.

A Day of 1600 Calories:

At least six servings of grains should be made up of whole grains or multigrains.

Three to four servings of vegetables are required.

4 servings of fruits

2 to 3 servings of low-fat or fat-free milk and milk products

3 - 4 servings (or less) of lean meat, poultry, and seafood

3 to 4 servings of nuts, seeds, and legumes each week

2 servings of fats and oils

Amounts of added sugars and sweets should be limited to no more than three servings per week.

An average of 2600 calories a day is recommended.

grains (whole or multigrain) = 10 to 11 servings

There are 5 to 6 servings of vegetables in this dish.

Five to six servings of fruits

Consuming three cups of milk and milk products containing no or low fat content

Meat, poultry, and fish make up six servings of lean protein.

1 serving of nuts, seeds, and legumes

3 servings of fats and oils

Sweets and added sugars can be consumed up to two times a day, but it is not necessary.

An average of 3100 calories a day is recommended.

12 to 13 servings of grains (ideally whole grains or multigrains)

At least six servings of vegetables are required.

Six servings of fruits.

3 to 4 servings of low-fat or fat-free milk and milk products

At least six to nine portions of lean protein (meat, poultry, and fish)

1 serving of nuts, seeds, and legumes

Four servings of fats and oils are equal to one cup of fat.

Sweets and added sugars can be consumed up to two times a day, but it is not necessary.